GHOST TOWNS
of the PACIFIC NORTHWEST

Your Guide to the Hidden History
of Washington, Oregon, and British Columbia

Text and Photography by Philip Varney

Voyageur Press

First published in 2013 by Voyageur Press, an imprint of MBI Publishing Company, 400 First Avenue North, Suite 400, Minneapolis, MN 55401 USA

The information in this book is true and complete to the best of our knowledge. All recommendations are made without any guarantee on the part of the author or Publisher, who also disclaims any liability incurred in connection with the use of this data or specific details.

We recognize, further, that some words, model names, and designations mentioned herein are the property of the trademark holder. We use them for identification purposes only. This is not an official publication.

Voyageur Press titles are also available at discounts in bulk quantity for industrial or sales-promotional use. For details write to Special Sales Manager at MBI Publishing Company, 400 First Avenue North, Suite 400, Minneapolis, MN 55401 USA.

To find out more about our books, visit us online at www.voyageurpress.com.

ISBN-13: 978-0-7603-4316-6
    Library of Congress Cataloging-in-Publication Data

Varney, Philip.
    Ghost towns of the Pacific Northwest : your guide to the hidden history of Washington, Oregon, and British Columbia / by Philip Varney.
        p. cm.
    Includes bibliographical references and index.
    ISBN 978-0-7603-4316-6 (sc)
    1. Northwest, Pacific--Guidebooks. 2. Northwest, Pacific--History, Local. 3. Ghost towns--Northwest, Pacific--Guidebooks. 4. Mining camps--Northwest, Pacific--Guidebooks. 5. Fortification--Northwest, Pacific--Guidebooks. 6. Northwest, Pacific--Pictorial works. I. Title.
    F852.3.V37 2012
    979--dc23
                        2012035068

Editors: Adam Brunner, Elizabeth Noll
Design Manager: Cindy Samargia Laun
Layout: Pauline Molinari
Cartograpy: Patti Isaacs, Parrot Graphics

Printed in China

10 9 8 7 6 5 4 3 2

Page 1: In Roslyn, Washington, several false-front buildings from about 1890 serve as classic examples of that era's architecture.
Page 2: Many of the graves in the Roslyn, Washington, cemeteries are for miners who came from eastern Europe.
Page 3: Diagonal slats adorn the facade of this former Shell service station in Antelope, Oregon.
Opposite page: A Masonic temple, built in 1907, stands along the main highway through Kerby, Oregon.

FOR GREG AND MARY ELLEN PSALTIS, ERICA PSALTIS, REID PSALTIS AND NAN ALLISON, AND KOSTA PSALTIS

CONTENTS

TO THE READER   8

INTRODUCTION:
THE GREAT MIGRATION   14

GHOSTS OF THE   Port Gamble   22
1 SEATTLE   Fort Flagler, Fort Worden, and Fort Casey   27
AREA   Wilkeson   36
                                 Roslyn   40
                                 Ronald   46
                                 Holden   49

GHOSTS OF   Molson   58
2 EASTERN   Bodie   62
WASHINGTON   Curlew   64
                                 Northport   66

GHOSTS OF THE   Greenwood   76
3 BOUNDARY   Sandon   85
COUNTRY   Retallack   90
                                 Ainsworth Hot Springs   92
                                 Fort Steele   94

GHOSTS OF THE   Skamokawa   102
4 GREAT   Grays River and Rosburg   104
COLUMBIA   Cottardi Station, Altoona, and Pillar Rock 107
                                 Knappton Cove   114
                                 Fort Clatsop   116
                                 Fort Stevens   120
                                 McGowan   123
                                 Fort Columbia   125
                                 Oysterville   130

5 **GHOSTS OF THE OREGON PLAINS**

Boyd, Dufur, and Friend	138
Wasco, Moro, and Grass Valley	144
Kent	152
Shaniko	156
Antelope	159
Mayville	162
Lonerock	165
Hardman	169

6 **GHOSTS OF NORTHEASTERN OREGON**

Whitney	179
Sumpter	181
Granite	186
Flora	192

7 **GHOSTS OF SOUTHWESTERN OREGON**

Jacksonville	197
Buncom	205
Kerby	206
Golden	209

ACKNOWLEDGMENTS	212
GLOSSARY	213
BIBLIOGRAPHY	216
INDEX	218
ABOUT THE AUTHOR AND PHOTOGRAPHER	224

TO THE READER

Ghost towns offer a fascinating and unique opportunity to explore the history of the West, providing a glimpse into a way of life now long gone. While most ghost towns in places such as California, Colorado, Nevada, or Arizona are remnants of once-booming mining communities, the Pacific Northwest's ghost towns have a more varied history. Only twenty-one of the fifty-four sites featured in this book were initially settled because of mineral wealth. Seventeen communities were farming towns, while eight were related to fishing, six to defending the United States, and two to logging.

I began prowling Oregon's back roads in search of ghost towns in 1982, but I didn't explore Washington's back country until 2000. I was really tardy venturing into British Columbia, first exploring for ghost towns there in 2003. Having now seen a small portion of that extraordinary province, I'll return—and often. I hope this book will inspire others to do so as well.

Ghost Towns of the Pacific Northwest is intended for people who love history, seek unusual experiences, and enjoy solitude. Some of the destinations in this book—out-of-the-way spots such as Holden, Washington; Sandon, British Columbia; and Flora, Oregon—may be unfamiliar even to natives of the area. Other sites attract thousands of visitors annually, such as Port Gamble, Washington; Fort Steele, British Columbia; and Jacksonville, Oregon. Chasing down the ghost towns of the Pacific Northwest will take you from the seacoast high into the forests of the Cascade Range. You will view the magnificent Columbia River as it passes through Revelstoke, British Columbia, to its first entry into the United States in Northport, Washington, and to its dramatic meeting with the Pacific Ocean near Astoria, Oregon. You will see the Pacific Northwest as you have never seen it before. That certainly happened to me.

The towns featured in this book are arranged geographically, so you can visit places in logical groups, beginning with some excellent sites within a day's trip of Seattle. The following chapters take you away from population centers and onto true back roads. Each chapter features a map of the area, a history of each town, a description of what remained at the site when I visited, specific directions to each site, and, naturally, photographs.

Café Cicely is a reminder that Roslyn, Washington, stood in for the fictional Cicely, Alaska, in the television series *Northern Exposure.*

A person new to ghost town hunting might tour the first entry in this book, Port Gamble, and wonder just what I consider a ghost town to be, because Port Gamble is a lovely, well-maintained, historic treasure. By my definition, a ghost town has two characteristics: The population has decreased markedly, and the initial reason for its settlement (be it mining, logging, farming, or fishing) no longer keeps people there. Port Gamble's sawmill has closed, and vacant lots attest to how many residences have disappeared. No one there today makes his living as a logger, and the population is a fraction of the community in its heyday. A ghost town, then, can be completely deserted, such as Bodie, Washington; it can have a few residents, such as Sandon, British Columbia; or it can have genuine signs of vitality, such as Sumpter, Oregon. But in each case, the town is a shadow of its former self. The three preceding examples were all mining towns, and their boom has long since passed.

To be included in this book, however, a town must have significant remnants. Fifty-four ghost towns are featured here, but I visited and eliminated 145 other sites (79 in Washington, 52 in Oregon, and 14 in British Columbia). Many were eliminated because so little of historic importance remains, but most were omitted simply because they are modern towns today.

The inclusion of military installations in a ghost town book may surprise some readers, but I have found that ghost town hunters also love old forts. Several of my previous books have featured installations that include historic remnants. Think of the six presented in these pages—three that guarded Washington's Puget Sound and three that stood sentry near the mouth of the Columbia River—as "ghost forts."

Ghost Towns of the Pacific Northwest encompasses two states and a portion of a province, so if you wish to visit all the sites in this book, you'll put significant miles on your vehicle. But I assure you that they will be some of the most enjoyable miles you will travel in the West. And, for the first time in all my books, I did not need four-wheel drive. I didn't even require a truck, although I used one.

I wrote my first ghost town book in response to my frustration with the way other such books are generally organized. I wanted a completely practical, informative guide that would fit comfortably on the seat of my truck. Some guidebooks I have followed in the West seemed to be written principally for armchair travelers. Unfortunately, some were written by armchair authors. I cringe when I realize that a book I'm using was written by someone who obviously hasn't personally observed what he is writing about. For this second edition, I revisited and rephotographed every site in this book in 2010 and 2011. The book's emphasis is on what remains in a town, not what was there in its heyday. I describe what to look for at each site, and in most cases I suggest walking or driving tours.

I also make recommendations about several museums and one commercial ghost town enterprise, British Columbia's Three Valley Gap Heritage Ghost Town (in chapter 3). My observations are candid, and I received no special consideration at such sites in the original edition of this book. On my return trip for the second edition, I did receive complimentary admission and permission to photograph both Three Valley Gap and Fort Steele, to take advantage of early light before the attractions opened (see acknowledgments). Otherwise, I paid for all attractions, and guides knew me only as another tourist. I received no special access to any other sites for photography; even at Three Valley Gap and Fort Steele, I did not go into any areas closed to tourists. I put away all my film cameras and lenses utilized in my first seven books and used a digital camera with only two zoom lenses. I did not use either a flash or a tripod. My purpose in doing this was that I wanted to take photos that any person with a camera could take. This is in contrast to some of my previous books in which either I or my photographer partners for three books, John and Susan Drew, paid for permits or were given special privileges because of what we were working on. I did not do that for this volume. If you like the photos I took, you can get the same shots I did.

When it comes to looking for photographic subjects, I suggest starting with graveyards. Almost every town has a cemetery, even if it has little else. A perfect example is in southern Oregon: The town of Sterlingville has completely vanished, but its cemetery remains. Some of my most enjoyable but poignant moments have come while walking around graveyards, since emotions are often laid bare on tombstones. To read the grief of parents in the epitaphs of their children is to see the West in absolutely personal terms. History comes tragically alive in cemeteries. In addition, headstones make wonderful photographic subjects, as you will see in this book.

To visit all of the sites in this book without frantically racing from one to another, I would estimate that you would need, heading out from Seattle, about five days for chapter 1.

For chapter 2, if you are going northeast from Chelan (the debarkation point for Holden, the last entry in chapter 1), you might need only two days, with a logical overnight at Kettle Falls.

I spent five days rephotographing chapter 3 in 2011, and I think you could do well in about the same time—perhaps a day less—if you start from either Osoyoos, British Columbia, or Kettle Falls, Washington.

The likely starting point for chapter 4 is Portland. You could visit all the sites with an overnight in a place such as Astoria, which is a town I love to visit every summer. But here's my advice: Take at least two days to enjoy this enchanting area.

Chapters 5 and 6 can be explored together rather conveniently. From Portland, I would estimate that you would need about a week, but I always tarry an extra night or two in Sumpter, Oregon, because it is such a wonderful place (see acknowledgments).

The principal town for exploring chapter 7 is Medford, although nearby historic (and delightful) Jacksonville has wonderful accommodations and restaurants. An overnight or two in either community is sufficient to visit this captivating area.

Why are we called to these places where so many have toiled and so many have been forgotten? My late friend, mystery writer Tony Hillerman, in the foreword to my New Mexico book, captured the answer: "To me, to many of my friends, to scores of thousands of Americans, these ghost towns offer a sort of touching-place with the past. We stand in their dust and try to project our imagination backward into what they were long ago. Now and then, if the mood and the light and the weather are exactly right, we almost succeed."

Our "touching-places with the past," however, are in immediate and long-term danger. Vandals tear up floorboards hoping for a nonexistent coin. Looters remove an old door with the vague notion of using it, only to discard it later. Thieves dislodge a child's headstone, heartlessly assuming no one will miss it.

These old towns are not only to be explored and photographed, but also to be protected and treasured. As you visit the places in this book, please remember that ghost towns are extremely fragile. Leave a site as you found it. I have seen many items on the back roads that tempted me, but I have no collection of artifacts. If you must pick up something, how about a fast food wrapper or a soft drink can? You must be a part of the preservation, not the destruction.

When I was doing fieldwork for my book on Colorado, I found the following notice posted in a lovely but deteriorating house. It eloquently conveys what our deportment should be at ghost towns and historic spots:

> Attention: We hope that you are enjoying looking at our heritage. The structure may last many more years for others to see and enjoy if everyone like you treads lightly and takes only memories and pictures.

Finally, a word to my Canadian readers: Please don't be offended by the title of this book. I realize that British Columbia is not in the "Pacific Northwest" of your great country. The title mostly reflects a simple way of describing the region. I have a special fondness for Canada, where I was warmly welcomed while doing fieldwork for this book.

— *Philip Varney*
Tucson

An unusual pyramidal rooftop caps this boarded-up two-story residence in Mayville, Oregon.

INTRODUCTION
THE GREAT MIGRATION

Oregon, Washington, and British Columbia are linked by more than mere geography. For thousands of years before the arrival of Europeans, indigenous people lived in their forests, fished their rivers and coastlines, gathered seeds in their vast inlands, and traveled their great waterways. When Europeans "discovered" the Pacific Northwest, four great nations laid claim to some or all of the combined territory.

Spanish seafarers Bruno de Heceta and Juan Francisco Bodega y Quadra were the first known Europeans to confirm claims on the region, when they reached the coast of the Pacific Northwest in 1775. The United States' claims were solidified when Captain Robert Gray was the first to sail into the Columbia River from the Pacific Ocean in May of 1792. Captain George Vancouver validated England's interests when he explored Puget Sound and the Columbia a month later. Mariners and fur traders from the north established claims for a fourth nation, Russia.

Spain and Russia eventually abandoned their stakes in the Northwest because of insubstantial documentation of claims and their pursuit of other colonial interests, leaving the region to England and the United States.

Following the Louisiana Purchase in 1803, Thomas Jefferson's Corps of Discovery, led by Captains Meriwether Lewis and William Clark, firmly established the United States' land claims in 1805 and prompted fur traders to explore the region further. In 1841, Congress passed the Pre-emption Act, which permitted males, widows, and female heads of families to claim 160 acres of public land for farming purposes. Two years later a westward movement, known as "The Great Migration," began. Over the ensuing three decades, more than three hundred thousand settlers, lured by the promise of a new Eden, took the two thousand-mile Oregon Trail west from Independence, Missouri.

The boundary between British Columbia and what would become Washington was established along the forty-ninth parallel in 1846, with the land north of the boundary belonging to England. Two years later, Congress established the Oregon Territory, which extended from the present-day northern boundary of Washington and the southern boundary of Oregon all the way east to the summit of the Rocky Mountains.

Even when you're miles away from Kent, Oregon, you'll be able to see the concrete grain silo (rear) and another behemoth made of wood.

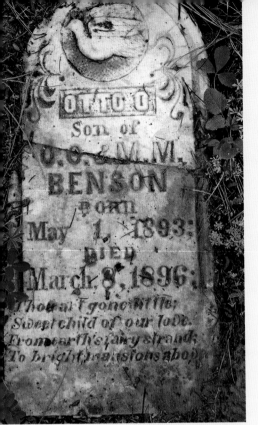

When the California Gold Rush began in 1849, many Northwest settlers headed south to the excitement. Others discovered, however, that they could make a profit off the rush without leaving the Oregon Territory by supplying California with wheat, flour, salmon, lumber, and shingles. Wheat was in such demand early in the 1850s that its price jumped from one dollar to six dollars per bushel in less than five years.

Washington became a separate territory in 1853, and its present boundaries took shape when the Idaho Territory was formed in 1863. Washington did not achieve statehood until 1889, whereas Oregon was granted statehood in 1859 and has seen no change to its boundaries since that time.

Otto Benson died when he was less than three years old. His epitaph, in the Blue Mountain Cemetery of Sumpter, Oregon, reads: *Thou art gone little; Sweet child of our love. From earth's fairy strand; To bright mansions above.*

North of the border, Vancouver Island became a crown colony of England in 1849. In 1858, gold was discovered in the Fraser River area, sparking an influx of at least twenty-five thousand settlers, most of them single men from Oregon, Washington, and the California gold fields. Although the Fraser excitement was short-lived, it sent prospectors looking elsewhere in British Columbia, resulting in subsequent strikes in the Cariboo, the Kootenay, and the Klondike. Originally known as New Caledonia, British Columbia began to have both urban and rural communities, and a considerable portion of the early settlers were Americans. In 1871, British Columbia became the fifth province of the Dominion of Canada, but its citizens voted to do so on the condition that a rail link from the east would be built.

Although mining lured many settlers to the Northwest, none of the strikes were long-lived enough to create permanent communities, except for the few towns that supplied coal. Farming, ranching, and the logging industry offered more stable incentives for immigrating to the area, especially when free land was offered under the Homestead Act beginning in 1862. And in the 1870s, the newly perfected canning process allowed the fishing industry to provide for more than a local market.

Nothing, however, influenced the populating of Oregon, British Columbia, and Washington more than the completion of railroads. The British publication *The Economist*, in the middle of the nineteenth century, noted that in the 1820s the speed a man could go unaided was about four miles per hour, "the same as Adam." By horse, it was up to about ten miles per hour for any distance. But *The Economist* went on to say that by the 1850s, a man could, by train, habitually go forty miles per hour and occasionally as high as *seventy*. Portland was connected to the Atlantic seaboard by rail in 1883. The Canadian Pacific Railway was completed between Halifax and

Vancouver in 1885. The Northern Pacific Railway entered Tacoma in 1887. All three political entities exploded in growth. To use Washington as an example, the territory's population in the 1880 census was 75,116. By the 1890 census, the newly formed Washington state was home to 357, 232 people. In 1897, Washington became the outfitting point for the Klondike Gold Rush, solidifying a link between the United States and Canada that remains economically and politically vital today.

St. Anthony's Catholic Church is a historic building (not a reconstruction) in Fort Steele, British Columbia.

Today, British Columbia, Washington, and Oregon have vibrant urban areas that are the jewels of the Northwest. But each of them has a highly skewed concentration of population. As a result, when you cross the Cascade Range, you enter rural areas that are far different from the commotion of Vancouver, Seattle, and Portland. It is in these areas where some of the best remnants of the past can be found.

To experience the Pacific Northwest's past, one can explore its historic remnants: the mining camps, prairie ghosts, and logging towns that were all but abandoned in search of more promising places. The tent camps have disappeared. The majority of wood-frame towns have vanished as well, having fallen to fire, vandalism, salvage, or the ultimate destroyer—gravity. Some delightful towns still exist, however, and the best are showcased throughout this book.

1

GHOSTS

OF THE

SEATTLE
AREA

YOUR PACIFIC NORTHWEST GHOST TOWN ADVENTURES begin with several sites within day trips of Seattle, including a delightfully preserved former lumber town, three forts that protected Puget Sound from naval attack, and three coal mining towns. Farther from Seattle is a copper-mining town virtually unchanged since the 1930s and isolated from the outside world—accessible only by a three-and-a-half-hour boat ride. Because these sites are in the most populous areas of Washington, they are not as "ghostly" as others in this book, but each displays only vestiges of its former life.

The Holy Trinity Orthodox Christian Church of Wilkeson, Washington, has an onion dome, a feature common on the churches of eastern Europe. Many of Wilkeson's coal miners came from that region.

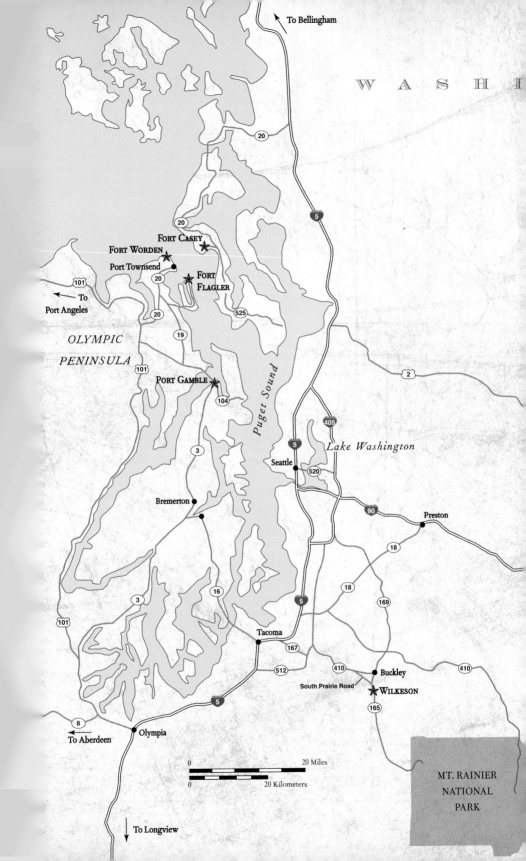

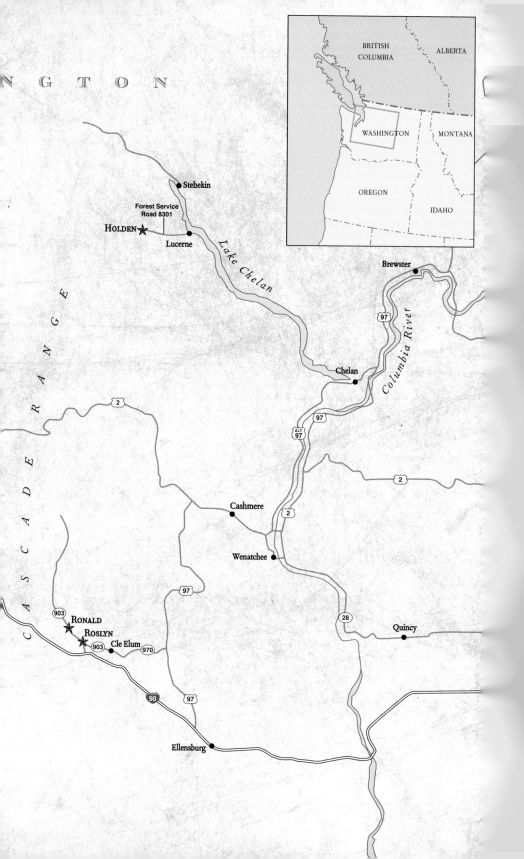

PORT GAMBLE

Port Gamble is one of the Northwest's most delightful communities. It was created as a company town in 1853 by Pope and Talbot, a lumber and shipping company originally formed in December 1849.

The year 1849 was, of course, the beginning of the California Gold Rush, which was to yield the largest concentration of gold in the history of the world. A. J. Pope, Captain William C. Talbot, and Cyrus Walker, natives of Maine, saw in the Gold Rush an opportunity for more than mineral wealth. They realized that San Francisco, the center of commerce for that rush, was about to surge in growth and prosperity. In 1853, Talbot and Walker led a maritime expedition up the Pacific Coast, eventually coming across huge supplies of timber, along with water deep enough for a sizable port, in Puget Sound. Pope and Talbot became experts at providing lumber for the booming economy in northern California.

Port Gamble's 1906 community center and post office is still the center of the action in town.

Built in 1916, Port Gamble's general store sells merchandise and houses two interesting museums.

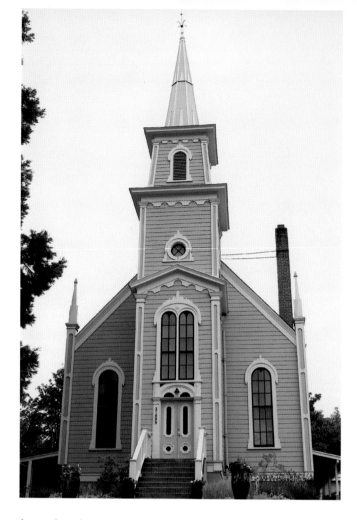

Port Gamble's St. Paul's Episcopal Church was modeled after a Congregational church in East Machias, Maine.

Pope handled sales and merchandising in San Francisco, while Talbot was almost constantly at sea, bringing Puget Sound lumber to the port of San Francisco.

Before Pope and Talbot invested in Puget Sound, a small settlement existed where Port Gamble would eventually develop. That community was originally known as Teekalet, an Indian word meaning "brightness of the noonday sun." Port Gamble was named in honor of Lieutenant Robert Gamble, a naval officer wounded in the War of 1812. The Pope and Talbot company town that grew on the site in 1853 was constructed to resemble East Machias, the hometown of the three Maine natives. The maple trees that line the main streets of Port Gamble today were brought as seedlings from East Machias.

Port Gamble was the site of Washington's oldest continuously operated sawmill until it closed in 1995. Today, only concrete foundations remain, and logs are merely shipped out by truck. Technically speaking, Port Gamble is no longer a "port."

WALKING AND DRIVING AROUND PORT GAMBLE

The largest building in downtown Port Gamble is the 1906 community hall, which once housed the post office, the telegraph and telephone headquarters, doctor's and dentist's offices, a barber shop, and an upstairs movie theater. The post office is still in operation.

South of the community hall stands the 1872 Franklin Lodge, which is the oldest active Masonic lodge in Washington, having been chartered in 1859. The building was never turned around when it was moved across the street in 1907, so its original front is now in the rear.

The most interesting building in town is the Port Gamble General Store and Office, which dates from 1916. A plaque in front of the store states that this was actually the fifth general merchandise in Port Gamble but the first in this location. The previous four were along the shore, because customers, such as settlers, Indians, sailors, and loggers, commonly arrived by boat.

Even the company-owned row houses are immaculately maintained in Port Gamble, one of Washington's best-kept communities.

In its present incarnation, the store not only sells merchandise, but it also contains two museums. The Of Sea and Shore Museum, located on two mezzanines above the first floor, offers a display of seashells and other marine items. In the basement, the Port Gamble Historic Museum chronicles the history of Pope and Talbot. Among the most attractive displays are re-created interiors of Pope's office in San Francisco, various sawmill operations, and portions of the 1906 Puget Hotel, which was severely damaged in 1962 by a storm and no longer stands.

Port Gamble's 1856 Buena Vista Cemetery, located west of the business district, does indeed have a "good view," as it stands on a hill offering a panorama of the town. The graveyard also contains many weatherworn markers. Not surprisingly, several of those buried here were from Maine, but others hailed from Canada, Ireland, England, Scotland, Sweden, Finland, and Germany.

On the south end of town stand several company houses and the community's loveliest building, the 1879 St. Paul's Episcopal Church, modeled after a Congregational church in East Machias. The church features a tall, graceful steeple with elaborately jigged woodwork.

WHEN YOU GO

Port Gamble is 24.5 miles north of Bremerton. Drive north from Bremerton on Washington Highway 3. When it intersects with Washington Highway 104 at the Hood Canal Bridge, go northeast on Highway 104 instead of crossing the bridge. You will enter Port Gamble in 1 mile. You can also reach the site by taking the Edmonds ferry to Kingston. Port Gamble is 8 miles northwest of Kingston on Washington Highway 104.

FORT FLAGLER, FORT WORDEN, AND FORT CASEY

As the population and commerce along the West Coast continued to expand during the last decades of the nineteenth century, Puget Sound took on an increasingly significant role in both commercial shipping and military defense. In 1896, the U.S. Government began construction of a massive shipbuilding dry dock in Bremerton. To prevent hostile ships from reaching that strategic shipyard or cities within the sound, the government built the "Triangle of Fire," three strategically positioned forts around Admiralty Inlet, the entrance to Puget Sound. Forts Flagler, Casey, and Worden—completed in 1899, 1900, and 1902, respectively—boasted an intimidating total of 106 guns. Many of them were mounted on carriages that allowed the cannons to rise up, fire, and disappear behind a concrete parapet, an innovation that made them state-of-the-art at the time.

None of the forts ever fired a hostile shot, but their formidable gun batteries served as powerful deterrents until World War I. When the United States entered that war in 1918, about half the artillery was removed from the forts and shipped to Europe, because the improved range and accuracy of warships' artillery, along with the possibility of airplane attacks, made these once-state-of-the-art guns ineffective in their "Triangle of Fire" positions.

Fort Flagler's hospital is painted a spiffy two-tone gray on its front and sides, but the back has a ghostly, unkempt look.

During World War II, the U.S. military held training activity at the forts, and antisubmarine defense nets were strung in the bay. By the end of that war, however, the military importance of the three former bulwarks of defense had ended. All three were decommissioned in 1953.

WALKING AND DRIVING AROUND FORTS FLAGLER, WORDEN, AND CASEY

If you are coming from Port Gamble, you will first encounter Fort Flagler, the southernmost of the three defenses. Constructed on the northern tip of Marrowstone Island, it was named for Civil War hero Brigadier General Daniel Webster Flagler. It became a state park in 1955.

Today Fort Flagler features a museum in the former quartermaster's depot, many historic buildings, and sweeping views of the inlet that the fort once defended. Some of the former quarters are used for vacation rentals, a hostel, and an environmental learning center. The largest and most intriguing building served as

Fort Worden's commanding officer's house, as you would expect, is the premier residence on officers' row.

The sitting room in the commanding officer's quarters at Fort Worden has been restored to its 1910 appearance.

the hospital, which at this writing is closed to the public. In fact, a volunteer told me rather ruefully that it is even closed to museum docents, who would dearly like to get a peek.

Seven gun batteries stand along the periphery of the fort, but only one actually has a weapon, as all the guns were removed by 1933. The Thomas Wansboro Battery features a gun brought for display purposes from the Philippines in 1963.

Fort Worden stands on the Quimper Peninsula and is the westernmost outpost of the "Triangle of Fire." It was named for Admiral John L. Worden, the commander of the Union's *Monitor* (the ironclad famous for its Civil War battle against the Confederate *Merrimack* in 1862). It is the only U.S. Army post named after a naval officer.

Fort Worden is so photogenic that it was chosen for the movie *An Officer and a Gentleman*. The fort's premier attraction today is the commanding officer's quarters, which has been restored to its elegant 1910 appearance. Nine other officers' residences, available as vacation rentals, stand west of the commanding officer's house.

The Coast Artillery Museum, housed in a former fort barracks, is located directly across from officers' row in Fort Worden.

The Admiralty Head Lighthouse at Fort Casey now serves as a museum.

The Fort Casey Inn, a bed and breakfast establishment, features junior officers' residences and the recently restored physician's quarters.

Also well worth exploring is the Coast Artillery Museum, located in a barracks across the parade ground from officers' row. Excellent models help visitors picture the remnants of Fort Worden's artillery batteries as they looked in their heyday. There are also displays of personal memorabilia, such as uniforms, letters, and even a dance card.

The old guardhouse, now a visitors' center, is west of the barracks. A military cemetery stands a short distance west of the visitors' center. The state park also features other military buildings, two campgrounds, walking trails, and the Point Wilson Lighthouse. Also on the grounds is the curious Alexander's Castle, which predates Fort Worden. A Scottish Episcopal minister, John B. Alexander, built it in the 1880s. When Fort Worden was constructed, the "castle" was used first as the post exchange and later as a tailor's shop.

Fort Casey, weather permitting, offers the clearest view of the "Triangle of Fire." When standing above the gun emplacements on Whidbey Island, you can see the positions of both Fort Worden, to the southwest, and Fort Flagler, almost directly south. From this vantage point, it is evident how the three forts posed a daunting challenge to any intruder into Admiralty Bay. Two ten-inch disappearing carriage rifles, brought from the Philippines in 1968 to replace the originals, stand on display along a self-guided interpretive walk.

Fort Casey, named in honor of Brigadier General Thomas Lincoln Casey, also features the 1890s Admiralty Head Lighthouse, a short distance west of the emplacements. The lighthouse last saw service in 1922, and it now houses displays of the fort's history.

The colonel's residence stands in solitary splendor at Fort Casey.

Inland from the gun batteries stand the other buildings of Fort Casey, including extensive barracks, commanding officer's quarters, and a gymnasium. The site belongs to Seattle Pacific University, and trespassing is prohibited, but the buildings can be viewed from the main road. The lovely former junior officers' quarters, now the Fort Casey Inn, are beyond that complex on the main road.

WHEN YOU GO

Fort Flagler is 29.3 miles from Port Gamble. From Port Gamble, return west for 1.2 miles on Highway 104 and cross the Hood Canal Bridge, following Highway 104 west for 6.7 miles. Turn north on Washington Highway 19 and continue for 10.7 miles, where Washington Highway 116 (at this point, Ness's Corner Road) goes east (with a sign for Fort Flagler). Follow Washington Highway 116 for 10.8 miles to Fort Flagler State Park.

Fort Worden is 20.7 miles from Fort Flagler. From Fort Flagler, retrace your route for 10.8 miles on Washington Highway 116 to Washington Highway 19. Turn right and proceed 3.5 miles, where Highway 19 dovetails into Washington Highway 20. Follow Highway 20 for 3.6 miles to the south end of Port Townsend, where a sign at a stoplight for Kearney Road directs you to turn left. Follow the small road signs north to Fort Worden State Park, a distance of 2.4 miles. Should you miss the small signs, here's what you will be doing: Follow Kearney until you take a right turn at Blaine. Follow Blaine to a T and turn left onto Cherry Street. Keep heading north on Cherry until you angle left onto Redwood Street. Take a right turn onto W Street, and then make a left turn into the Fort Worden State Park Conference Center at Cherry Street.

To reach Fort Casey: Take the ferry from Port Townsend to Whidbey Island. Immediately after leaving the ferry, turn left. In 0.4 of a mile you will enter Fort Casey State Park.

Note: *During the peak summer season, advance reservations on the Port Townsend to Coupeville (Whidbey Island) ferry are usually essential. Go to www.wsdot.wa.gov/ferries.*

PORT TOWNSEND

Port Townsend is a modern, bustling community with fast-food chain restaurants and all manner of modern conveniences. Actually, that only describes its southern outskirts. At its heart, Port Townsend is one of the nation's loveliest Victorian towns, and as long as you are visiting nearby Fort Worden, you should take the time to look around.

Port Townsend's 1890 Jefferson County Courthouse is a marvelous creation of brick and stone.

Port Townsend was founded in 1851 as a seaport for the area's fishing and lumber industries. The promise of a railroad in the 1880s led to tremendous overbuilding, and the community became a semi-ghost town when the railroad never materialized. Fortunately, the fabulous Victorian structures that had been erected for the anticipated prosperity were not demolished. Port Townsend remains, as guidebooks will tell you, "Washington's Victorian Treasure." A free driving-tour brochure is widely available in town.

When you are done visiting Fort Worden, instead of retracing your way south all the way to Washington Highway 19, turn left on Lawrence Street and head up the hill that stands above downtown Port Townsend. This is Uptown, where almost every residential street has lovely restored homes, and several commercial and civic buildings overlook downtown as well. Be sure to drive east to Jefferson Street, where the magnificent red-brick and sculpted-stone Jefferson County Courthouse stands.

Completed in 1892, it was designed by Washington's first prominent architect, Willis A. Ritchie (1864–1931).

Water Street is the main thoroughfare down at the edge of Puget Sound. For about five blocks on Water, one ornate, cornice-topped brick masterpiece stands shoulder to shoulder with another, each trying to surpass the other in elegance and, in some cases, pomposity. One example that I would call over-the-top Victorian is the 1889 Hastings Building, on Water Street at Taylor Street. It features an elaborate cast-iron facade and bay windows projecting over the sidewalk below. But it is hardly the only delightful building, most of which date from 1889. The earliest date I noticed is on the wooden former Customs House, at Tyler and Water Streets, which was erected in 1878. Incidentally, Taylor and Tyler Streets are one block apart, perhaps leading to occasional postal confusion.

Find yourself a parking space (not always easy to do on summer weekend afternoons) and stroll the four- or five-block downtown.

The best overall view of Port Townsend will be on your way to Fort Casey, as the ferry to Whidbey Island offers a panorama of downtown and the lovely residences, churches, and the hilltop courthouse.

The Hastings Building, built in Port Townsend in 1889, features an elaborate display of oriel windows on the second and third floors.

WILKESON

Wilkeson is a reminder that not all mining towns exist because of precious metals. The town was founded in 1876 when the Northern Pacific Railway laid tracks to extensive high-grade coal deposits discovered two years earlier. The community was named for Samuel Wilkeson, secretary of the railroad's board of directors. Mining began in 1879, and in 1885 the Tacoma Coal and Coke Company built 165 brick ovens to heat coal into hotter-burning coke.

A second industry began when the railroad started quarrying sandstone for use as ballast. The sandstone later was used for buildings after it was discovered that the stone did not absorb water, unlike virtually all sandstone. The quarry provided blocks for numerous structures, including the dome of the Washington State Capitol in Olympia.

The nation's declining demand for coal and coke led to Wilkeson's decline in the 1930s.

Wilkeson's town hall and library was built using local sandstone in 1923.

WALKING AND DRIVING AROUND WILKESON

When you approach Wilkeson from the north, you will pass its cemetery on the left, a half-mile before you enter the town itself. The gravestones are rather close together, and many plots have concrete borders. The overall effect is a cemetery with a distinctly "old world" look to it.

Beyond the cemetery, two large sandstone columns—with a huge log sitting atop them stretching across the road—welcome you to the quarry and coal town of Wilkeson. The community's center features several attractive brick buildings, including the Wilkeson Grocery, which resembles the stores of California's '49er Gold Rush with its porch over the sidewalk.

South of the grocery is the brick, two-story 1910 Carlson Block, and, across the street, a two-story 1910 brick structure that houses the Fraternal Order of Eagles. Both buildings are rhomboids, with their fronts paralleling the street, but their sides sitting at about eighty-degree angles.

The stately Wilkeson School, constructed in 1913 of local sandstone, is on the National Register of Historic Places.

The 1880 Washington Hotel in Wilkeson was at one time a brothel. It also served as a gin mill during Prohibition.

Two doors south of the Eagles' building is a single-story 1923 sandstone edifice that serves as a combination city hall and library. The attractive Washington Hotel stands across the street.

At the south end of the business district, Railroad Avenue veers off to the left. There you will find the 1913 Wilkeson School, a large, three-story sandstone building featuring a cupola and two stately columned entrances. It is on the National Register of Historic Places.

Beyond the school, the remains of fifty-two coke ovens stand in two back-to-back rows behind a set of bleachers. Encroaching blackberry vines make the ovens almost disappear.

The residential section of town features some attractive homes and one lovely church. The 1910 Holy Trinity Orthodox Christian Church is on Long Street near Hill Street. Its graceful blue "onion dome" reflects the architecture of eastern Europe.

The small community of Carbonado, another coal mining company town, is two miles south of Wilkeson on Washington Highway 165 and is worth a visit.

Wilkeson's cemetery, with its many concrete borders, has a distinctly eastern European look to it.

WHEN YOU GO

From Fort Casey, on Whidbey Island, there are multiple ways to travel to Wilkeson. The shortest, fastest route is to go from Clinton (on the southeast end of Whidbey Island) to Mukilteo by ferry and then head south toward Seattle. You could also return to Port Townsend by ferry and then head south toward Tacoma. You could take the Kingston ferry (southeast of Port Gamble) to Edmonds, which is north of Seattle. You can even take a land route north to Fidalgo Island and then head east to Mount Vernon, where Interstate 5 will take you south toward Seattle.

Your goal, whichever route you take, is Puyallup, a thriving community south-east of Tacoma. Wilkeson is 18 miles southeast of Puyallup. From Puyallup, head north on Washington Highway 167 until Washington Highway 410 branches off heading east toward Sumner and Yakima. Follow Highway 410 for 5.9 miles and turn right on South Prairie Road East. You will drive for 4.1 miles, just skirting the small town of South Prairie. Turn left on Pioneer Way East and go for 2.1 miles. When it intersects with Washington Highway 162, keep right. Keep right when Washington Highway 165 goes south only three hundred feet from your last turn. Follow Highway 165 for 2.7 miles to Wilkeson.

ROSLYN

Roslyn is a very charming town. So charming, in fact, that it had its own television show. From 1990 until 1995, Roslyn posed as Cicely, Alaska, on the quirky series *Northern Exposure*. Even a cursory visit to the town reveals why it was selected as the location; a longer look will convince you that this is one of Washington's genuinely special communities.

Roslyn came to life in 1886 when the Northern Pacific Railway began mining the area's abundant coal. The community was named by Logan M. Bullitt, vice president of the railroad's subsidiary coal company, who supposedly chose the town's name because a woman he was trying to impress lived in Roslyn, New York.

The railroad's mining company recruited extensively in Europe for experienced miners, and over time people from twenty-eight nations settled in Roslyn. In 1888, hundreds of African Americans were brought in from the southern and eastern United States to mine coal. What these new workers did not know was that they were being used as strikebreakers, and their arrival generated hard feelings

The former city hall and library, with the former fire department located in the basement in between them, combine into a kind of governmental triplex.

that lasted for many years. Despite the initial hostilities, many African Americans remained in the area, and tensions eventually subsided. In fact, in 1975 Roslyn became the first town in Washington to elect an African American mayor. In the peak coal production years, from 1901 until the 1920s, Roslyn mines surpassed two million tons per year, and the town's population exceeded four thousand people. But in the 1930s, more widely available electricity and fuel oil lessened the demand for coal, and production began to decline. Mines began closing in 1936, and by 1949 Roslyn was quietly heading to ghost town status. The last mine held on until 1963. Today it is estimated that 283 million tons of coal, four-fifths of the original seams, still remain.

WALKING AND DRIVING AROUND ROSLYN

Washington Highway 903 becomes First Street as you enter Roslyn, and the intersection of First and Pennsylvania Avenue marks the center of town. This is a good place to park your car for a walking tour. The quiet community of Roslyn became a National Historic District in 1978. The named streets in town apparently honor states where famous mining bonanzas occurred—Alaska, Nevada, Utah, Arizona, Idaho, Washington, Pennsylvania, Dakota, Montana, Oregon, Colorado, California, and Wyoming. Notably absent is one of the great coal states, West Virginia.

The old company store, which operated from 1889 until 1957, stands on the northeast corner of Pennsylvania and First. A sign on the brick-and-wood-truss building says "Northwestern Improvement Company," referring to the firm that purchased Roslyn and the coal mines in 1898. *Northern Exposure's* fictitious radio station, KBHR 57 AM, "The Voice of the Last Frontier," occupies the eastern portion of the store.

Directly in front of the general store is the Coal Miners' Memorial and Statue. A plaque lists the dates of Roslyn's major mining disasters.

Across the street from the company store stands the former Cle Elum State Bank, built in 1910, which now houses Roslyn's government offices. There you may obtain a flyer with directions for a helpful walking tour of the town and a second sheet that highlights the locations used in *Northern Exposure*.

Standing across First Street from the old bank is the 1899 Brick Tavern, reportedly Washington's oldest operating saloon. One of its highlights—if that's the right word—is a "gutter" spittoon with running water.

Across the street from the tavern are three wooden, false-front commercial buildings followed by another group of three, all constructed roughly between 1888 and 1890.

An unusual combination city hall–fire station–library stands on First Street south of Pennsylvania Avenue. The 1902 building is a kind of government triplex, with identical stairways for the former city offices and the library—between them sits the basement fire department and its driveway.

Unrestored, original residences from Roslyn's coal-mining days are getting harder to find. Only a few remain.

The residential areas of Roslyn are graced by many restored former company homes. Mixed into the neighborhoods are attractive churches, including the 1887 Immaculate Conception Catholic Church at B Street and Idaho Avenue and the 1900 Mount Pisgah Presbyterian Church at Idaho and First Street.

The remarkable Roslyn cemeteries comprise one of the finest historic graveyards in this book, and certainly the best in this chapter. The expanse of these cemeteries, twenty-five in all with an estimated five thousand graves, is simply staggering. A small portion of the cemeteries comes into view as you approach Memorial Avenue, but many of the most interesting sections are partially hidden by trees and overgrowth. To reach these exceptional graveyards, take Pennsylvania Avenue west to Fifth Street, which leads to Memorial Avenue.

You can explore the City Cemetery, the oldest graveyard, dating from 1887; two areas for veterans; and many fraternal graveyards, such as Moose, Eagles, Odd Fellows, Knights of Pythias, Red Men, Foresters, and Masons. There are several cemeteries for immigrant lodges, which were formed to provide accident and death benefits as well preserve the heritage for citizens of Italian, Croatian, Lithuanian, Polish, and Serbian backgrounds.

These three false-front buildings in Roslyn, built in about 1890, are classic examples of commercial structures from that era in the American West.

Roslyn's City Cemetery features fine old headstones and elaborate wrought-iron fences.

On my second visit to Roslyn in 2003, I saw a gentleman working at a lovely gravesite, almost a tiny park within the Masonic section. I went over to compliment him on his careful tending. He introduced himself as Will Craven, and we began talking about the memorial that he had erected for his son, Tom, who had died two years earlier fighting the Thirtymile Fire in the Chewuch River Canyon in north-central Washington. All four firefighters who perished are memorialized in Roslyn, but only Tom is buried there. As Mr. Craven spoke lovingly about his son, I saw on the marker that he had died two years before—*to the day*—on July 10, 2001. When I apologized that I might be intruding on Mr. Craven's day of grief, he told me that he was glad I had come by, that there was a memorial service near the site of the firefighters' deaths, but that he just didn't feel up to attending. He said that I had given him a chance to talk about his son, and that was something he needed to do. Incidentally, this was in the African American Masonic Cemetery. Mr. Craven was born and raised in Roslyn in one of those families who succeeded despite racial difficulties. His grandparents, parents,

cousins, brother—and son—are all buried in the cemetery. I mentioned earlier that Roslyn, in 1975, was the first town in Washington to elect an African American mayor. That mayor was Will Craven.

WHEN YOU GO

Roslyn is 94 miles northeast of Wilkeson. From Wilkeson, follow Washington Highway 165 for 4.3 miles north to Buckley. Continue north on Washington Highway 410 for 3 miles to Enumclaw. From Enumclaw, take Washington Highway 169 to Maple Valley, a distance of 15 miles. Head northeast on Washington Highway 18 for 12 miles to Interstate 90. Turn onto I-90 heading southeast and drive 55 miles to Exit 80. Go north for 3.1 miles, where you will enter a roundabout onto Washington Highway 903, which leads you to Roslyn in 1.2 miles.

RONALD

Ronald is an often-overlooked community northwest of Roslyn. Although Ronald cannot compare to its more luminous sister, it remains well worth exploring. The town was named for Scotsman Alexander Ronald, one-time superintendent of the coal mines of the Northwestern Improvement Company. The town shares much of its history with Roslyn, because many of the coal mines were located between the two communities.

A local resident who grew up in Ronald (see acknowledgments) during its heyday told me that during Prohibition the miners made more money in the bootlegging business than in their mining jobs. He said the Slovaks were the whiskey providers, while the Italians were specialists in winemaking. He related that once a still blew up and took out an entire block. He also told me that his grandfather didn't receive an actual check for wages for several years because he was always in

Ronald's schoolhouse features covered staircases leading to the main entrance on the second floor.

This one-time company house in Ronald stands in its original, unrestored condition. It was last occupied in the 1950s.

hock to the company for his house, groceries, and other necessities. It reminds us of the famous line from the song "Sixteen Tons": "Saint Peter, don't you call me, 'cause I can't go / I owe my soul to the company store."

WALKING AND DRIVING AROUND RONALD

Evidence of the coal mines that brought Ronald to life stand east of town. Ronald features some company houses similar to those in Roslyn, a one-stall firehouse with a cupola, and a large, two-story community center. The best building in town, on the northwest corner of Third Street (one block east of Second Street, which is Washington Highway 903 in Ronald) and Atlantic Avenue, is the tan, two-story clapboard schoolhouse, which features matching covered staircases that students would take up to the elevated main entrance at the center of the building. The school offered grades one through eight. Northwest of the school on Third Street are several company houses, including one on the southwest corner of Third Street and Pacific Avenue that has remained unoccupied and virtually unchanged from Ronald's mining days.

WHEN YOU GO

Ronald is 1.8 miles northwest of Roslyn on Washington Highway 903.

THE CHELAN COUNTY MUSEUM AND PIONEER VILLAGE AT CASHMERE

A logical stop between Ronald and the last entry in this chapter, Holden, is the Chelan County Museum and Pioneer Village at Cashmere. The museum's village contains seventeen historic buildings that give visitors a close-up look at life in frontier Washington. Among the structures, which date from as early as 1872 and are all furnished with period pieces, are several residences, a post office, a schoolhouse, a barbershop, a blacksmith shop, a jail, a saddle shop, an assay office, a hotel, a saloon, a print shop, and a millinery shop. A doctor and dentist's office has a particularly fine exhibit of professional equipment.

The Chelan County Museum and Pioneer Village is in Cashmere, 54 miles northeast of Cle Elum on U.S. Highway 97. For directions between Ronald and Holden, see the Holden entry, which follows.

An 1898 cabin (left) has been turned into the Mission Hotel at the Pioneer Village in Cashmere. Beyond the hotel are a doctor and dentist's office, the 1891 Weythman Cabin, and a print shop.

HOLDEN

Holden is unique. Of the more than six hundred ghost towns and mining camps that I have visited, it is the only one that was saved because it was donated to a church. It is also the only one so remote that you can access it only by boat. And because of that donation and that isolation, Holden stands virtually as it was when built in the 1930s.

Holden was named for James Henry "Harry" Holden, who discovered promising ore deposits in 1896. The remoteness of the site delayed mining development until 1929, when intermittent work began by the Howe Sound Mining Company of Canada. In 1937, mining began in earnest. A sawmill was erected, and the trees that were cleared for the townsite were used to construct the town of Holden in 1938, twenty years after Harry Holden's death.

The village was located in a spacious canyon safely between two known avalanche zones. The Swiss chalet–style architecture was a vast departure from the

This skeletal mill reminds us that, although Holden is now a religious retreat, at its founding it was a copper mining town. This mill remnant will eventually be removed from the site.

The former hotel at Holden now houses the dining hall, bookstore, post office, and guest laundry of a religious retreat.

usual, dreary buildings of a company town. In 1939 the *Wenatchee Daily World* hailed the new camp as "the model mining town of the world." The same newspaper article states what is still true today: "You'll feel like you're more on a college campus than in a mining town."

West of town was a community called Winston Camp, erected on Forest Service land by Winston Brothers contractors, who built 101 small houses for married housing. That community does not survive. Neither does Honeymoon Heights, where young mining engineers brought their wives to live high above the Holden townsite, near the original mine workings.

The Howe Sound Company carefully screened applicants to find those who could live for extended periods in relative isolation. The company provided varied activities, such as basketball leagues, dances, and holiday celebrations. The community was so self-sufficient that it minted its own tin fifty-cent pieces, used in Holden's Peter Rabbit grocery store (which came into being after World War II). The coins were even accepted in taverns in Chelan. Liquor was available by ordering from a bus driver who traveled the route from Holden to Lucerne (a small community on the shore of Lake Chelan) daily and then sent the order via boat to Chelan. Public drunkenness, however, resulted in immediate dismissal.

Holden's population peaked at about six hundred as the copper, silver, zinc, and gold operation became the biggest producer of any metal in Washington between 1938 and 1957. Former Holden residents generally remember life there as happy, far away from the troubles of the world. The average resident left Holden only once a year. Consider, for example, that people lived there for the duration of World War II without personal telephone access to the outside world. (There was a phone line, but it was only for company business.)

After production of more than $100 million in ore, about 70 percent of that from copper (and $550 million at today's prices), mining ceased in 1957. The town was put up for sale for $100,000. There were no takers, however, and the Howe Sound Company transferred the title of Holden to the Lutheran Bible Institute for one dollar in 1960. The ghost town of three years came back to life as a retreat center.

Holden's chalets originally housed the mining company's upper management.

WALKING AROUND HOLDEN

A relaxing, scenic, forty-three-mile, three-and-a-half-hour boat ride from the town of Chelan takes you up Lake Chelan to the boat dock near Lucerne, a tiny lakeshore community that features cabins that formerly stood in Holden. A school bus then climbs from the dock up a steep, twisting dirt road that rises over 2,100 feet, most of it gained in the first couple of miles. The bus ride takes you eleven miles in about forty-five minutes into Holden Village. There you will retreat from the modern world. The feeling of serenity is palpable.

You will arrive in front of the former hotel—now the dining hall, post office, store, guest laundry, and registration center. Surrounding the hotel are seven buildings, six of which originally were miners' dormitories. The seventh was a hospital that once had an operating room, x-ray facility, two private rooms, and a four-bed ward.

Southeast of the hotel is the Village Center—the former Recreation Hall—which features several step-back-in-time attractions: a first floor featuring a combination gymnasium–dance hall–movie theater–auditorium and an ice cream parlor, and a basement containing a barber shop, a pool hall, and a four-lane bowling alley (with no automatic pinsetters).

Immediately east of the Village Center stands the former schoolhouse. Across the street from the school is a lane that leads to thirteen attractive chalets, twelve of which served as the residences of the mining company's upper management. The other home was reserved for guests.

A short walk west of town takes you to the remnants of the mining operation—its waste dumps, tailings piles, and the unsalvaged skeleton of the old mill, all of which will eventually removed from the site. On your way to the mining detritus, right after you cross a bridge over Railroad Creek, you'll see a small, roofed information kiosk that has a cross-cutting of a huge ponderosa pine. Right behind that are two log cabins still very much habitable, with a small, concrete holding pond immediately adjacent.

Holden today has a year-round resident population of about sixty, but each year they are joined by almost a thousand volunteers and about seven thousand guests. The guest capacity at any one time is more than four hundred people. Summer is the busiest season by far, although winter retreats are offered as well, despite Holden's yearly average of 251 inches of snow.

Holden's former Recreation Hall, now called Village Center, contains several 1930s attractions, including an old-time ice cream parlor and a basement bowling alley and pool hall.

The surrounding scenery—in the mountains of the eastern Cascade Range, with glaciers and pine-filled canyons—is stupefyingly beautiful. The mining scars are the only blemish to the beauty, but they remind visitors why this canyon was settled in the first place.

You do not have to be a Lutheran to visit Holden, nor are you required to attend any religious service—and there certainly is no proselytizing effort. The ferry and bus schedules, however, do make it necessary to stay overnight. The silence at night—free of automobiles, television, and late-night revelers—made my two mid-July visits, in 2003 and 2011, two of the most memorable and relaxing I've had in my ghost town travels.

WHEN YOU GO

Chelan is 103 miles from Ronald. From Ronald, return to Roslyn on Washington Highway 903 and continue into neighboring Cle Elum, 3 miles southeast of Roslyn. Take Washington Highway 970 east from downtown Cle Elum for 12 miles to its junction with U.S. Highway 97. Follow that highway for 86 miles to the town of Chelan, on the south end of Lake Chelan. You will then leave your car and take the Chelan–Lucerne–Stehekin boat to Lucerne, the port for Holden. Holden is 11 miles west of Lucerne. Reservations at Holden are a necessity (the cost includes meals and bus transportation to and from Lucerne). For information, go to www.holdenvillage.org or write Holden Village, HC00— Stop 2, Chelan, WA 98816.

2

GHOSTS

O F

EASTERN
WASHINGTON

THE GHOST TOWNS IN THIS CHAPTER take you away from densely populated places of Washington and into some relatively isolated, lovely areas containing apple orchards, forests, and rolling hills. These ghost towns have a much more abandoned look than those in chapter 1. In addition, you will spend much of your time near the United States–Canadian border, which will give you an opportunity to explore some ghost towns on the other side of the boundary in the following chapter.

Old Molson is reflected in the front door window of the Molson State Bank in Molson, Washington.

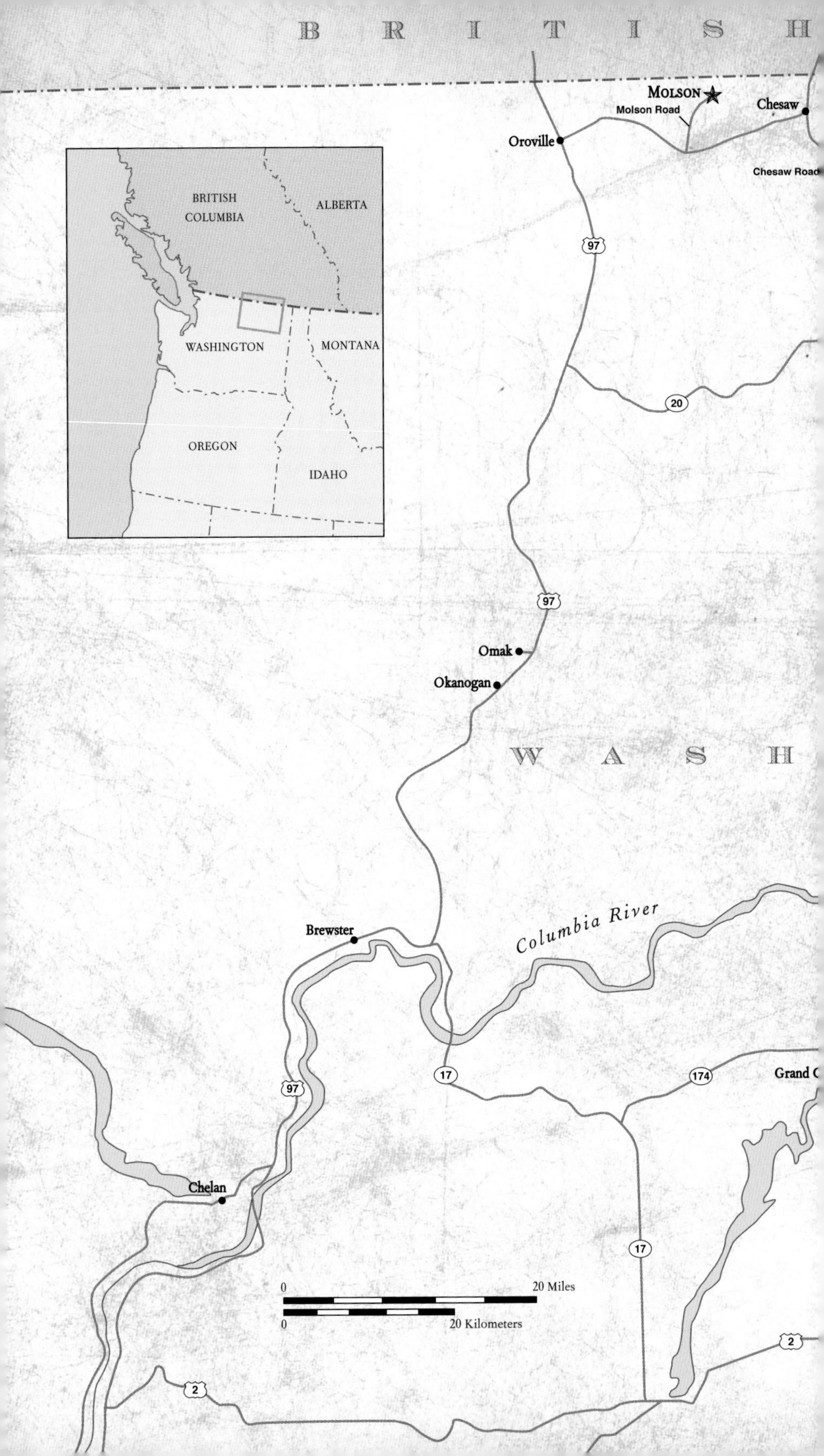
B R I T I S H
Molson
Molson Road
Chesaw
Oroville
Chesaw Road
97
BRITISH
COLUMBIA
ALBERTA
WASHINGTON
MONTANA
OREGON
IDAHO
20
97
Omak
Okanogan
W A S H
Columbia River
Brewster
17
174
Grand C
97
Chelan
17
0
20 Miles
0
20 Kilometers
2
2

MOLSON

Molson was founded as a mining and speculative enterprise in 1900 by promoter George Meacham with the financial backing of Montreal banking and brewing entrepreneur George Molson. The community, which Molson himself never saw, almost died within a year, but homesteading pioneers resurrected the site. When a farmer claimed that the whole town was part of his homestead, Molson was moved a half-mile north. The arrival of the Great Northern Railway in 1906 further legitimized the town.

The community, which had a peak population of about seven hundred, became a trading and commercial center, serving not only north-central Washington but south-central British Columbia. Molson once featured hotels, five churches, three fraternal organizations, a cafe, a confectionery, and two pool halls.

When area mines played out, Molson's decline began. When the railroad tracks were taken up in 1935, the town's demise was assured. The town lost its post office in 1967, its final step toward becoming a ghost town.

Molson is a little more than a mile south of the U.S.– Canadian border, and this old sign in Old Molson sternly reminds us of that.

The Molson State Bank contains teller cages, a safe, and, oddly, a printing press. The downturned horseshoes indicate Molson's luck has run out.

WALKING AND DRIVING AROUND MOLSON

As you enter town from the south, the first site you will see is Old Molson. The Molson State Bank, which features an angled front door, tellers' cages, and a 1906 safe made in Cincinnati, is the best of several historic buildings grouped closely together. A 1908 homesteader's log cabin nearby is furnished with a Majestic Stove for cooking, an ice box, a washing machine, a heating stove, a dining table with chairs, and a bed. Scattered around the buildings are various farming and mining implements.

Northeast of Old Molson is Central Molson, where the 1914 former schoolhouse, now a museum, is the principal attraction. The building served grades one through twelve from 1915 until 1962, when high school students were bused to Oroville. The school closed entirely two years later. I recommend taking your time walking through this wonderful museum, because much of the school looks as it did when it closed in 1964. I remembered, to my amazement, some of the high school textbooks that line the shelves. The school's basement, which contains the gymnasium and bleachers, features a collection of marksmanship medals and an amazing display of carefully crafted hand tools. You enter the gymnasium down an aisle between the wonderful, but probably uncomfortable, wooden bleachers.

A classroom inside the Molson schoolhouse has many delightful touches, including three vintage lunchboxes, two (foreground and center) featuring Mickey Mouse and Goofy in a school bus, and one (far right) made to look like a television set with Bugs Bunny and Sylvester on the screen.

The Molson Trading Company has a creative mural featuring "townspeople" inspecting the "merchandise" in the "windows."

Across from the schoolhouse stands a tidy brick building with a sign proclaiming it "Molson Trading Company, Gen'l Merchandise." The store has a clever mural painted on its front showing the reflection of a street scene.

The tiny Molson Cemetery stands on a hill seven-tenths of a mile south of Old Molson. At the southeast end of the cemetery, you might pause to pay respects to Harry A. Sherling (1899–1997) and Ethel Sherling (1901–1987). Harry Sherling was the driving force behind the preservation of Old Molson and the creation of the museum. Note that he was three years short of living in three centuries, not a common thing to do. When you are looking at a signboard showing locations of graves, you are at Range Seven; they are buried in Range Four.

WHEN YOU GO

Molson is 112 miles northeast of Chelan, your debarkation point to Holden, the last entry in chapter 1. From Chelan, drive 97 miles north on U.S. Highway 97 to Oroville. In Oroville, go north on Main Street (Highway 97 in town) to Central Avenue. Turn right on Central and proceed 0.3 of a mile to Cherry Street. Cherry Street becomes Chesaw Road in 0.2 of a mile. Follow Chesaw Road for 9.1 miles and turn left on Molson Road. From that point, follow Molson Road for 4.9 miles to Old Molson, on your right.

Note: Chesaw Road was formerly called Oroville–Toroda Creek Road and is still so labeled on some maps.

BODIE

Bodie was founded in 1896 by prospectors looking for gold at the mouth of Bodie Creek, which empties into Toroda Creek. The log town featured a general store, restaurant, livery barn, blacksmith shop, and residences. When gold was discovered north of Bodie, the townsite was moved one mile to its present location along Toroda Creek. The second Bodie had a sawmill, so most of the town was constructed of cut lumber rather than logs, a step that indicated both sophistication and permanence.

The secondary placer deposits of Toroda Creek led to the discovery of primary deposits. A mill was erected, and an estimated $1.3 million in gold was extracted between 1903 and 1940 from area mines, such as the Elk and the Golden Reward. Chicago's Wrigley brothers, who made their fortune in chewing gum, owned the Golden Reward from 1902 until 1911.

WALKING AROUND BODIE

The sparse remains of Bodie straddle Toroda Creek Road. At this writing a dozen deserted buildings stand at the site. The largest is a two-story board-and-batten residence, which once also served as a school. Across the street stand a log cabin and another board-and-batten house that have an unusual connecting hallway between them.

These two residences in Bodie have an unusual hallway connecting them.

This board-and-batten residence in Bodie also once served as the town's schoolhouse.

WHEN YOU GO

Bodie is 31.9 miles southeast of Molson. From Central Molson, return 5.4 miles to Chesaw Road. Drive 10.8 miles east to Chesaw, passing a ghostly deserted farmhouse at 6.7 miles from the Molson Road turnoff. In Chesaw, take a right to continue on Chesaw Road for another 13.5 miles. At that point, Chesaw Road ends in a T at County Highway 9495, also known as Toroda Creek Road. Turn south on Toroda Creek Road and proceed 2.1 miles to Bodie.

CURLEW

In 1896, Guy Helphrey and J. Walters constructed a store at a ferry crossing near the junction of the Kettle River and Curlew Creek. (A curlew is a snipe-like bird that once was common in the vicinity.) The town that grew near that store took the name of the creek when a post office was granted in 1898. Curlew prospered as a supply point for area mines. The town's prominence seemed assured when the Great Northern Railway arrived just after the turn of the twentieth century, but, unfortunately, the mines were already playing out.

Local lore says that, during Prohibition, barrels of whiskey were bootlegged into the United States by putting them in the Kettle River at Midway, British Columbia, and letting the contraband float down to Curlew. That practice is now celebrated on Barrel Derby Day (the first Sunday of every June), when a barrel (now, alas, merely containing water) is placed in the Kettle River at Ferry—which is on the U.S. side of the border south of Midway. Attendees of the event make their best guesses as to when the barrel will arrive. The event is a fundraiser for local civic groups and typically includes a pancake breakfast, a parade, and other activities.

Curlew's old schoolhouse lost its bell but gained a certain amount of clutter.

The Ansorge Hotel in Curlew once had Henry Ford as a guest.

WALKING AND DRIVING AROUND CURLEW

Today Curlew is a somnolent town (except on that first Sunday in June) that features several interesting and attractive buildings. Right before you enter the main town, you'll be on Boulder Creek Road. Partially hidden behind another building on your right is the former Curlew School, so keep an eye out for it. You'll enter the town proper on River Street looking right at Curlew's best building, the Ansorge Hotel. This 1906 building featured pressed-tin siding and jutting, second-story, corner oriel windows that appear rather like the eyes of one of those lizards that can see in all directions. The Ansorge claimed Henry Ford as one of its guests in 1917, and now serves as a museum open on weekends.

Beyond the hotel, at the corner of River and Ferry Streets, is the Curlew Store. It isn't that photogenic outside, but it is a treat to explore inside, with its creaky floors and old display cases. Built in the winter of 1901–1902, the general store once also housed the post office and a pharmacy, and the second story still serves as a residence.

East of the store on Ferry Street is Church Street heading north. Follow that to the Catholic St. Patrick Mission. A Presbyterian church with an attractive offset bell tower stands northeast of the Ansorge Hotel.

WHEN YOU GO

From Bodie, drive north on Toroda Creek Road (County Road 9495) for 12.3 miles, at which point it ends at West Kettle River Road. A left turn would take you north to Midway, British Columbia. Instead, follow West Kettle River Road for 9.1 miles southeast to Curlew. You will come in on the south end of town. Cross Washington Highway 21 onto Boulder Creek Road. A left turn on River Street takes you into Curlew.

NORTHPORT

I was tempted to write off Northport when I drove into town in 2003, because the buildings along the highway are modern and nondescript. Then I took to the back streets and found that, although Northport is a living town, it does have interesting ghost town remnants. But when I returned in 2011 for this second edition, two of those remnants were gone. Northport has regressed from a minor site to a very minor site, and that might affect your decision of whether or not to visit Northport.

The first settlers came to the Northport area in 1876. Named because it was the country's northernmost port on the Columbia River, Northport boomed beginning in 1892 with the construction of a sawmill, the publication of the *Northport News,* and the initiation of ferry service across the Columbia River. The Spokane Falls & Northern Railroad reached town a year later, along with "a lady of elegant leisure," who was subsequently going to Spokane to "lay in a supply of girls," according to the *News.* Northport became an important smelter site, principally for ore from British Columbia. The town also became a vital shipping point for quarried stone and lumber.

The town declined in the 1920s with a series of setbacks. The Northport Smelting and Refining Company smelter, erected in 1897 to process zinc, lead,

Northport's Kendrick Mercantile Building stands along Columbia Avenue down by the railroad tracks in the older part of town.

and silver, closed after World War I and was dismantled in 1922. In addition, a prolonged drought allowed forest fires to consume huge stands of timber, closing all the lumber mills. Finally, a huge smelter in Trail, British Columbia, about fifteen miles north of Northport, was discharging enormous amounts of sulfur dioxide, sickening Northport's livestock, stunting crops, and poisoning the soil so that the burned forests failed to regenerate.

WALKING AND DRIVING AROUND NORTHPORT

The best buildings in Northport today stand on Columbia Avenue, near the railroad tracks. The avenue's southernmost building, originally the Liberty Hotel, served for many years as the post office, with a Masonic Lodge upstairs. When I revisited the town in 2011, the building was a pile of rubble. North of that structure stands the empty, two-story Kendrick Mercantile Company. Up the street is a combination library and museum, which originally was a bank. All the buildings likely date from the 1910s.

On the corner of Summit Avenue and Third Street stands another fine brick building, Beard's General Merchandise. Sirens on its roof and red front doors show a later incarnation as the town's firehouse, but it currently is used for storage.

The ruins and smokestack of the Northport Smelting and Refining Company smelter once stood north of town. A city park that was adjacent to the ruins has been expanded, and the ruins no longer exist. It is a loss for ghost town enthusiasts, but it is a definite gain for the citizens of Northport.

WHEN YOU GO

Northport is 91.2 miles northeast of Curlew, and there are three main ways to get there. I recommend the most dependable, which also happens to be the longest of the three—but only by about ten minutes. From Curlew, drive 19 miles south to Washington Highway 20. The delightful town of Republic is only 3 miles west of that junction, and I suggest taking a look. Kettle Falls is 43.6 miles east of Republic on Washington Highway 20, but the turnoff to Northport is just 0.9 of a mile west of town. I'd take that short distance to visit Kettle Falls, my favorite place to stay in northeastern Washington. Northport is 33.3 miles northeast of Kettle Falls on Washington Highway 25.

SHERMAN AND GOVAN

Sherman and Govan are two minor ghost towns far removed from the main sites in this chapter, but each features picturesque buildings, and I have found the detour well worthwhile on both of my visits.

The 1898 Presbyterian church at Sherman features a lovely steeple that rises gracefully from its entrance.

Sherman comes as a surprise. You're driving up a dirt road that doesn't show much ghost town promise when you enter a small, picturesque former farming and ranching community that features the Potlatch Grange Hall, erected in about 1928, and the lovely, well-cared-for 1898 Sherman Presbyterian Church. Unfortunately, the former schoolhouse for Ridge District No. 23 has collapsed. Its roof sits atop the ruins of the structure near the southwest corner of Sherman Road and Sage Hen Draw Road.

Adjacent to the church is a tidy cemetery. The oldest grave I found is for Mary A. Spencer, born in 1870, "beloved wife of James Franklin Spencer." She didn't reach her eighteenth birthday.

Sherman was founded by homesteaders in the early 1880s and apparently named for the Sherman family, as George Sherman was the postmaster in 1885. The town declined after the turn of the twentieth century and lost its post office in 1905.

The Potlatch Grange, now in disuse, was built around 1928.

The Potlatch Grange Hall and the Presbyterian church at Sherman form a classic scene of prairie ghosts.

Govan (go-VAN) was a sheep and cattle ranching community named for an engineer on the Washington Central Railroad, a branch line of the Northern Pacific Railway that was extended through the area in 1890. Today the town features two vacant residences and outbuildings and one highly photogenic structure: the 1905 clapboard school that features wood shingle siding up to about wainscoting level. The school, which closed in 1942, is deteriorating badly at this writing. Please treat this fragile, skeletal structure with respect. I have never stepped inside it, and I suggest that you don't either.

From Northport, return to Kettle Falls. Drive south from Kettle Falls on Washington Highway 25 for 81.4 miles to Davenport. From Davenport, go 25.5 miles west on U.S. Highway 2 to Sherman Draw Road, which heads north. Take that road for 4.2 miles until it ends in a T at Sherman Road. Take a right onto Sherman Road, which veers to the left and reaches Sherman just 1 mile north of that T.

To reach Govan, return to U.S. 2. Turn right and head to Wilbur, 4.3 miles west. Continue through Wilbur and drive 4.7 miles west on U.S. 2 to Govan Road. Turn south and proceed into the townsite. You also might want to examine Almira, 6.9 miles southwest of Govan on U.S. 2, which is a living community with a decaying town center featuring several two-story brick buildings.

Govan's 1905 schoolhouse is one of Washington's most spectral ghost town buildings.

wonderful Fort Steele, a heritage town that rivals similar but more well-known historic sites in the United States such as California's Columbia (featured in my book *Ghost Towns of California*) and Colorado's South Park City and Montana's Nevada City (both showcased in my book *Ghost Towns of the Mountain West*).

An authentic tin sign points the way to Hotel Bellevue in Three Valley Gap, British Columbia.

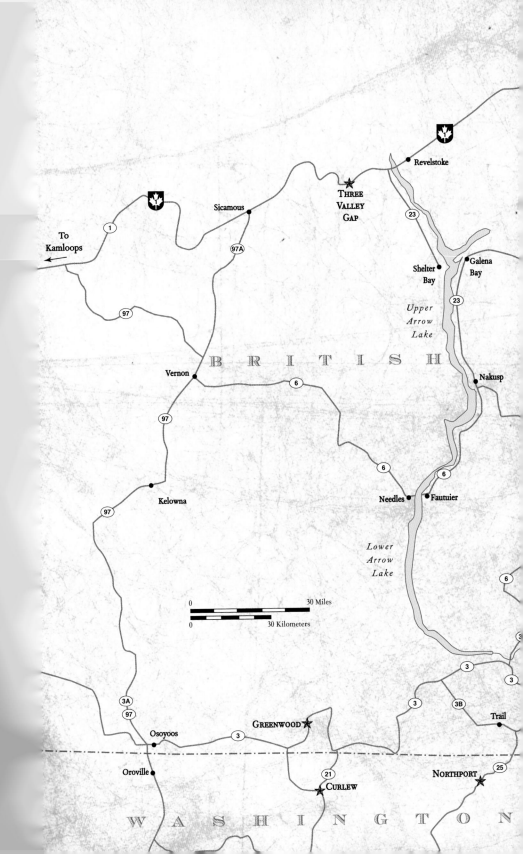

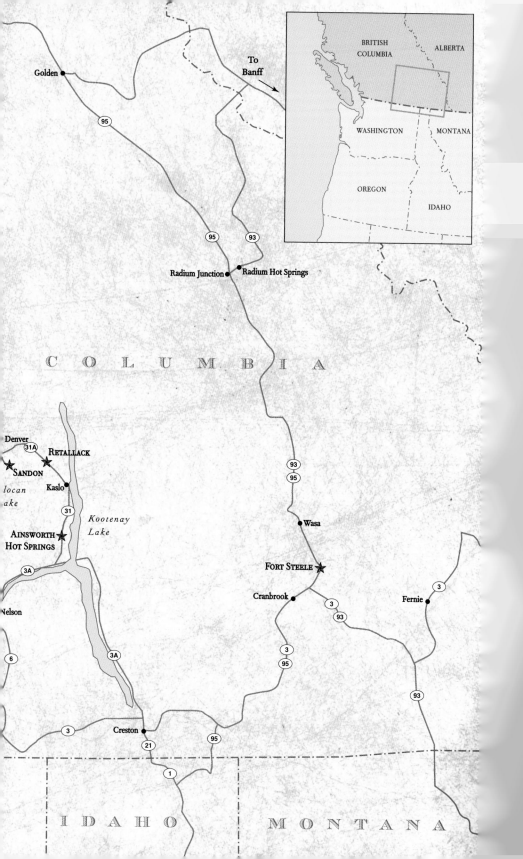

GREENWOOD

Greenwood came into existence in 1895, when entrepreneur Robert Wood concluded that it would be an ideal place for a trading center for the mining camps springing up along Boundary Creek. He purchased a ranch owned by Otto Dillier and hired men to begin clearing and developing a townsite that was named Greenwood, for a mining town of the same name in Colorado.

A year later, Greenwood had a sawmill, a hotel, a general store, two assay offices, a bakery, a laundry, and plans for an opera house. When the town was incorporated in 1897, Robert Wood became the town's first mayor, chosen by acclamation.

As Greenwood expanded, a competing settlement, Anaconda, developed immediately west of town. But Greenwood remained the dominant community, and by 1898 it could boast of six hotels, eight general stores, and a population of about 3,500 people. Despite repeated ravages by fire, Greenwood prospered until world copper prices fell dramatically in 1900. The town did not die, but its glory days

Greenwood's 1902 Gulley Block was Internment Building No. 3 when it was used to house Japanese Canadians during World War II.

The lovely Windsor Hotel, erected in Greenwood in 1899, features oriel windows on both its second and third stories.

were behind it. In 1935, the already depressed economy of Greenwood took another downward turn when the worst of Greenwood's many fires destroyed several downtown buildings; another major conflagration followed only three months later.

By World War II, Greenwood was nearly a ghost, with about two hundred citizens. At that time, Greenwood and several other fading towns in the interior of British Columbia became the sites of Japanese internment centers for more than twenty-two thousand people, about three-quarters of whom were Canadian-born or naturalized citizens.

Canada was not alone in this mass population movement: In the United States, more than 120,000 people of Japanese descent were relocated to internment camps as well. Of course, the enemy in World War II also included Germany and Italy, but citizens of those backgrounds were not singled out in either the United States or Canada. (To learn much more about this period of Canada's history, stop by the Nikkei Internment Memorial Centre at 306 Josephine Street in New Denver, which is on your way between Greenwood and Sandon, the following entry in this chapter.)

This fine 1899 brick commercial building, which stands next door to Greenwood's Windsor Hotel, serves as a coffee house and bakery. The restored 1955 Chevrolet sedan delivery is a delight to any car enthusiast.

Greenwood was the first town to receive Japanese internees, 1,203 in all. Cramped, bitterly cold conditions awaited them as up to twenty families shared antiquated living, kitchen, and bathroom facilities in buildings that were essentially firetraps.

In contrast to the prevailing prejudice and suspicion rife in both Canada and the United States, Greenwood's mayor, W. E. McArthur, tried to accommodate his new residents as best as possible. He encouraged them to revive the moribund town, and community functions and festivities bloomed despite the difficult circumstances.

Immediately after World War II ended, the United States closed its centers and allowed the detainees to return, if they chose, to the formerly restricted West Coast. In Canada, however, the internees were given the choice of being dispersed to towns east of the Rockies, where discrimination and menial, low-paying jobs awaited them, or being deported to Japan, which was a war-ravaged country most of them had never seen. Mayor McArthur invited his Japanese and Japanese Canadian citizens to stay, and when the restrictions were finally lifted—incredibly, not until 1949, four years after the war ended—many chose to remain in Greenwood.

WALKING AND DRIVING AROUND GREENWOOD

As you enter Greenwood from the south, you will immediately see evidence of its mining past: a looming brick smokestack (containing almost two hundred fifty thousand bricks) and the slag pile of the 1901 B. C. Copper Company Smelter. The smelter operated until 1918, when postwar prices for copper plummeted.

The principal thoroughfare in Greenwood is, appropriately, Copper Street. As you enter downtown, two three-story wood-frame structures dominate the west side of Copper. The more ornate is the 1899 Windsor Hotel, which reportedly boasts the longest-operating pub in British Columbia. The 1908 Pacific Hotel next

The Barrett House, built around 1902, is one of Greenwood's most striking residences.

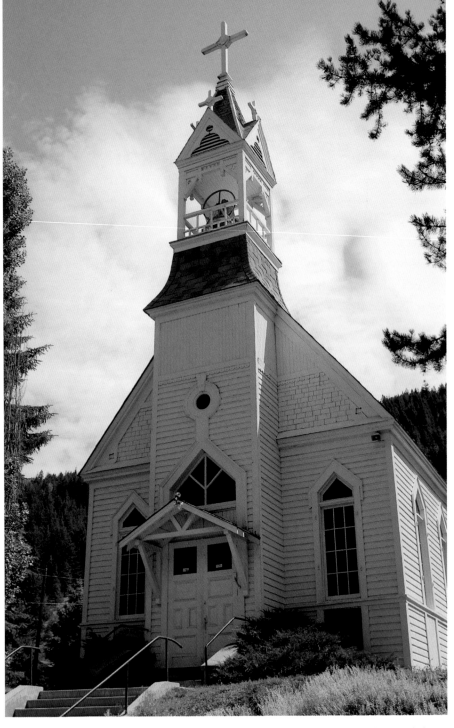

The Sacred Heart Catholic Church was home to an order known as the Atonement Friars, who came to Greenwood when the Japanese Canadian community arrived in 1942.

door was Internment Building No. 1, home to more than two hundred "guests" during World War II. A sign on the building in 2003 indicated that the upper floors still have remnants of that occupation, but that sign was not there in 2011.

Across the street is the two-story brick Gulley Block, built in 1902. Formerly Internment Building No. 3, it is now a community theater, library, and home to the Royal Canadian Legion.

Several buildings on Government Street, one block east of the town's center, are worth a look, including the Barrett House, built about 1902, which stands at 326 Government Street. North of that residence are the lovely, clapboard Greenwood City Hall, the fire department across the street from city hall, and the post office, all located near the intersection of Government and Deadwood Streets.

On Church Avenue, one block east of Government, stand, not surprisingly, two churches—St. Jude's Anglican Church, which features a detached bell tower, and, at the corner of Church and Wood Streets, the 1897 Sacred Heart Catholic Church.

To visit the town's cemetery, go north from downtown on the main highway for 1.6 miles, passing a curious tunnel off to the right that has lost the hill it formerly burrowed through. Turn left on Boundary Creek Road and drive for 0.8 miles (stay left when Jewel Lake Road veers to the right). The cemetery will come clearly into view on your right.

Many Japanese are interred in the cemetery; all of the graves I saw were of people who chose to remain in Greenwood long after their internment ended. Incidentally, there is no Japanese section in the cemetery. Their graves are intermingled with others.

WHEN YOU GO

Greenwood is 52.4 miles east of Osoyoos, British Columbia, on Provincial Route 3, the Crowsnest Highway.

__Note:__ Distances in this chapter will be given in miles for the simple reason that most of the people using this book will have automobile odometers measuring in miles. To convert miles into kilometers, simply multiply the miles by 1.6: for example, 11 miles x 1.6 = 17.6 kilometers. To convert kilometers into miles, multiply the kilometers by 0.625 (17.6 km x 0.625 = 11 miles).

THREE VALLEY GAP HERITAGE GHOST TOWN

Three Valley Gap is well out of your way as you proceed through the historic towns in this chapter. But if you have time, I certainly recommend a visit. The scenery is spectacular, and the site, which is near the location of a now-vanished nineteenth-century mining and lumber town, features some extraordinary relocated buildings.

In an ideal world, ghost town enthusiasts would like to visit original, well-preserved buildings standing in their abandoned townsites. Unfortunately, abandonment too often means vandalism, decay to the point of collapse, or destruction in the name of "progress."

Three Valley Gap's heritage ghost town, part of the Three Valley Lake Chateau, is the triumphant result of the preservation efforts of entrepreneur Gordon Bell, his wife Ethel, and their children, who moved outstanding buildings to a location where they should stand indefinitely. These buildings almost certainly would no longer exist had they been left where they originally stood. Mr. Bell died in 2007, but the family still runs the Three Valley Lake Chateau and its attendant enterprises.

Three Valley Gap's ghost town, which would more accurately be described as a pioneer village, is the principal attraction among fine

Both the C. B. Hume General Merchants and the Railway Standard Watchmaker & Jewellery Store are reproductions at Three Valley Gap, but they are highly representative of classic false-front stores.

The Hotel Bellevue was saved from almost certain collapse and reassembled board by board at Three Valley Gap.

collections of private railroad cars, automobiles, and countless other items, including one of the Brill electric trolley buses formerly stored at Sandon (see the following entry). I suggest spending at least a couple of hours at the site.

A good example of a structure that likely would not have survived in its original location is the 1898 Hotel Bellevue, a massive, three-story clapboard building that was in operation in Sicamous, thirty-three miles west of Three Valley Gap, until 1952. The hotel featured fifty rooms but only three bathrooms—and only one of those contained a bathtub! Purchased by Gordon Bell in 1964, the hotel was carefully dismantled board by board to be erected at Three Valley

A 1908 schoolhouse from the town of Carlin was moved piece by piece and reassembled at Three Valley Gap in 1965.

Gap. Ethel Bell told me that it took almost two years just to get all the furniture moved out of the building. The hotel features its original bar and a dining room that showcases Hotel Bellevue china.

To visit Three Valley Gap, head northwest from New Denver (the town nearest Sandon, the next entry in this chapter) to Nakusp on Provincial Route 6 and on to Galena Bay on Route 23, a total distance of 58.5 miles. Take the free ferry from Galena Bay across to Shelter Bay and go north 33.6 miles to Trans Canada 1, at the west end of Revelstoke. Three Valley Gap is 11 miles west of that intersection. Revelstoke, incidentally, features a fine railroad museum.

A glorious cash register catches the morning light behind a storefront window inside the Railway Standard Watchmaker & Jewellery Store in Three Valley Gap.

SANDON

Virginia native Johnny Harris set out in 1892 to prospect in the area of Slocan Lake. He and two partners purchased existing claims and eventually made a fortune in silver. He then staked another claim and created a town at the junction of Carpenter and Sandon Creeks, naming the town after the latter creek, which in turn had been named for French Canadian prospector John Sandon. Harris built a power plant on Carpenter Creek, and before long Sandon was the commercial hub of the silver excitement known as the Silvery Slocan. The town grew to a population of about five thousand and featured twenty-nine hotels, twenty-eight saloons, a city hall, brothels, a soft drink plant, three breweries, a cigar factory, three churches, and a bank. Both the Canadian Pacific and the Great Northern Railways extended tracks into Sandon.

Floods, fires, and avalanches plagued the community, set as it was in a narrow canyon, but it was the fall of ore prices in the early 1900s that began the demise of Sandon. There was a brief revival during World War I, but the Great Depression doomed the town.

Sandon's Slocan Mercantile, dating from 1900, currently serves as the town's museum.

Bottles rescued from Sandon's remains stand in the window of the Slocan Mercantile, along with some glass insulators.

During World War II, Sandon, like Greenwood, temporarily came back from ghost town status as "home" for 920 relocated Japanese Canadians.

Town founder Johnny Harris, who remained in Sandon from boom to bust, died in Sandon in 1953. Two years later a flash flood took most of the town down-river into Slocan Lake. A local resident, surveying the ruins of the town, declared, "It's good Mr. Harris isn't here to see his town go!"

Canadian Pacific Railway's locomotive No. 6947 stands near Sandon's city hall.

WALKING AROUND SANDON

Today, Sandon should look much better than it does. The town features a three-story city hall, a general store, a still-functioning powerhouse, and several old residences. It stands in a picturesque canyon with Carpenter Creek cascading through. Unfortunately, two large, two-story plywood-shrouded hulks presently mar the overall panorama. This strange sight is the result of an effort, begun in 1993 by the provincial government, to reconstruct the demolished Atherton and Burns buildings. A local resident told me in 2003 that when the person behind the project failed to win reelection, construction ceased and the buildings were simply covered. As a result, the work done in 1993 is deteriorating, and there seem to be no plans to finish the project. These two "boxes" blemish what should be one of Canada's best ghost towns. My sincere hope is that by the time you visit Sandon, the Atherton and Burns buildings, along with an ice cream parlor between them, will be beautifully completed—but I doubt it. When I revisited Sandon in 2011, the unsightly boxes remained.

You will encounter a rather surreal sight when you enter Sandon on Slocan Star Street. A fleet of Brill electric trolley coaches, dating from the 1950s, stands seemingly ready to head out and pick up passengers on the Seymour and Pender or the Mayfair routes. The only thing lacking is overhead electricity. They were moved to Sandon from Vancouver for eventual restoration and placement in

Sandon's city hall has been in restoration floor by floor since 1989. Perhaps the scaffolding, visible in the center of the building, doesn't reach the third floor? In my two visits, eight years apart, fresh paint still hadn't reached any higher.

museums, but they have stood idle for years with little apparent progress. Nearby stands a derelict Canadian Pacific Railway 0-8-0 locomotive, dating from the early 1900s, ready to haul its freight cars out of Sandon. The Kaslo & Slocan Railway, completed in 1895, carried silver ore from Sandon to Kaslo, a town you will go through on your way to Ainsworth Hot Springs (see page 92). The Great Fire of 1910 (referred to in the next entry, Retallack) destroyed the railroad.

The Sandon City Hall, erected in 1900, is a logical place to start a tour of Sandon, as it is the first structure you will come to along Slocan Star Street. The building, privately owned, has been in the process of major renovation since 1989, and photos inside attest to the amount of work accomplished. Unfortunately, the exterior painting that was incomplete in 2003 showed only minor progress when I revisited in 2011. In the city hall you can purchase a helpful walking tour map.

The 1900 Slocan Mercantile, the only brick building constructed in Sandon, stands next to the uncompleted government restorations and currently serves as the Sandon Museum.

On the southeast end of town stands the 1916 Silversmith Hydroelectric Generating Station (open for tours), the successor to an earlier plant on the same site. The generators are currently producing about one-quarter of the plant's original capacity—but still enough to supply all of Sandon's needs. It is the oldest continuously operating plant in western Canada, and Sandon reportedly was the first town in British Columbia to be completely electrified.

WHEN YOU GO

From Greenwood, continue east on Provincial Route 3 for 85 miles until it intersects Provincial Route 6 at Castlegar. Take Route 6 north for 61 miles to New Denver.

From New Denver, drive 5.3 miles east on Provincial Route 31A, the road to Kaslo. Turn right (southeast) onto a good gravel road clearly marked for Sandon, which is 3.6 miles from that turnoff.

RETALLACK

Retallack and Ainsworth Hot Springs (see following entry) would not be in this book if they weren't conveniently located on the way from Sandon to marvelous Fort Steele, the final entry in this chapter. Since they are on your way, stop to give them both a look.

Seven years after the discovery of an 1891 silver strike that was claimed under the name of Whitewater, banker and promoter John L. Retallack—who formerly had been a sergeant in the North West Mounted Police—raised the capital to open mining operations.

In 1910, a fire that began in New Denver, more than twelve miles away, roared east through Whitewater, destroying the town and mining buildings. Fortunately, the townspeople had been given sufficient warning, so they hid in a mine tunnel, and all were spared.

When the town was rebuilt, it was renamed in honor of Retallack, who had essentially founded it. Its prosperity peaked during World War II, but production ceased in 1952.

DRIVING THROUGH RETALLACK

Retallack currently is a mere spot along the road between New Denver and Kaslo, with two standing wood-frame buildings, one of which appears to have been a residence, the other likely a dormitory.

WHEN YOU GO

From Sandon, return 3.6 miles to Provincial Route 31A and turn northeast. Retallack is 7 miles from that turnoff.

Only two buildings stand as reminders of the once-vibrant town of Retallack.

AINSWORTH HOT SPRINGS

In 1882, George Ainsworth and two other U.S. citizens prospected the shores of Kootenay Lake. They found, in addition to promising gold deposits, a natural hot springs, so they filed claims on 160 acres that encompassed both. The town that developed there became known as Hot Springs Camp, but it was changed to its present name when Ainsworth was granted sole title to the property. Modest gold production lasted from 1889 until 1930.

DRIVING THROUGH AINSWORTH HOT SPRINGS

Ainsworth Hot Springs is a minor site with one attractive wooden building—the single-story J. B. Fletcher General Merchandise, built in 1896 by Montanan Henry Giegerich. The general store was first managed and then owned by J. B. Fletcher from 1912 into the 1970s, and the building houses a museum at this writing. A wonderful three-story hotel, the Silver Ledge—also built in 1896—still stood when I first visited in 2003, but was destroyed in a suspected arson in June 2010.

The hot springs are the major attraction at the community today, but another drawing point is the fine view of Kootenay Lake, British Columbia's third-largest natural lake.

The snow-capped mountains around Kootenay Lake provided a stunning setting for the town of Ainsworth, as shown in this photo from the late nineteenth century. (British Columbia Archives, B-05428)

J. B. Fletcher's store is the only historic building at Ainsworth Hot Springs after a fire in 2010 destroyed the Silver Ledge Hotel. Mere days before I took this photo, a gust of wind blew away the canvas awning that was attached to the framework over the store windows and front door.

WHEN YOU GO

Ainsworth Hot Springs is 30.1 miles southeast of Retallack. From Retallack, head 16.4 miles east on Provincial Route 31A to Kaslo, a charming town with many historic build-ings. Kaslo, like Greenwood, New Denver, and Sandon, also held Japanese Canadian internees during World War II. Ainsworth Hot Springs is 13.1 miles south of Kaslo on Provincial Route 31.

FORT STEELE

Fort Steele is the ghost town gem of southern British Columbia. Developed as a provincial heritage town beginning in 1961, the combination settlement and military post is a collection of beautifully restored buildings along with a few unrestored structures with a true ghost town look.

Before being restored, Fort Steele had two incarnations. In 1864, the spot was known as Galbraith's Ferry, where Irishman John Galbraith offered a ferry service to cross the Kootenay River on the way to the Kootenay Gold Rush, which began four miles away on Wild Horse Creek. In 1887, the town's second life began when the North West Mounted Police constructed a fort at the site, known as Kootenay Post, with Samuel Benfield Steele as superintendent. In 1888, John Galbraith himself renamed the town in honor of Steele, and Fort Steele became a thriving community of 1,500 residents. Although he objected to the name change, Steele would well deserve the honor: He later became a Canadian national hero as a steadfast enforcer of the law during the Klondike Gold Rush of 1897 to 1898, a commander in South Africa's Boer War (1899 to 1902), and a major general in World War I.

Fort Steele's Government Building retains its original, incommodious jail cells.

The interior of Fort Steele's Doctor Grice's Painless Dentistry office features implements that hardly look, well, painless.

Nearby strikes of silver and lead in the 1890s increased the town's prosperity and importance. But in 1898, Fort Steele was bypassed by the Canadian Pacific Railway, which went instead through Cranbrook, nine miles to the southwest. Merchants, professionals, and even the provincial government offices relocated near the new railroad. Furthermore, steamboats no longer plied the Kootenay River, and the Wild Horse Creek gold fields had played out. Fort Steele, once known as the "Capital of the East Kootenay," was moribund.

WALKING AROUND FORT STEELE

Fort Steele helps you to leave the present behind by requiring that you leave your automobile behind at the entrance. From there you stroll through uncrowded streets, step into shops selling various merchandise, peer into store windows displaying new old-stock items, and tour through homes, churches, and even a Masonic hall—all filled with period furniture and memorabilia.

The City Bakery and the International Hotel and Restaurant are reconstructions of former buildings at Fort Steele, while the *Prospector* newspaper office (far right) is typical of buildings of the era but never stood in the town.

Store clerks and other employees dress in period costumes. When I was photographing the town on my second visit in 2011, I came upon two gentlemen in period attire on a street corner. They stepped aside to let me pass and acknowledged me by tipping their hats, in a nineteenth-century demonstration of courtesy and good manners. I, hatless, gave them a slight salute, touching my first two fingers to my brow, feeling very much out of place. Hatless during Queen Victoria's reign? The very idea!

You can take railroad and wagon rides (the latter pulled by handsome Clydesdale horses) and also view exhibitions of such activities as plowing fields and sawing logs using antique equipment.

Fort Steele's historic one-room schoolhouse features all manner of school appurtenances, along with a map of Canada and a portrait of Queen Victoria.

This panorama of Fort Steele was taken from the second-story stairway of the Coventry Opera House. Left to right are St. Anthony's Catholic Church, the International Hotel, the *Prospector* newspaper office and book store, and the Pioneer Drug Store.

Of the fifty-nine structures in town, thirty-six are historic and seven are reconstructions of buildings that once stood at Fort Steele. The remaining sixteen are representative of structures common to provincial villages of the era.

One of the most uncommon is a 1967 reconstruction of the Wasa Hotel, which once stood in Wasa, about twelve miles northwest of Fort Steele. Within this large, two-story replica, featuring expansive porches and delicate railings, is a museum with outstanding displays and memorabilia. It is also air-conditioned, something you will appreciate if you visit Fort Steele during eastern British Columbia's occasionally baking summer.

WHEN YOU GO

Fort Steele is 141 miles southeast of Ainsworth Hot Springs. From Ainsworth Hot Springs, drive south for 9.1 miles on Provincial Route 31 to Balfour and take the free ferry 5.4 miles across Kootenay Lake. From the eastern shore, take Provincial Route 3A for 48.8 miles south to the junction with the Crowsnest Highway, Provincial Route 3, just north of Creston. From that junction, follow Provincial Route 3 for 67.8 miles to Cranbrook. From downtown Cranbrook, take Provincial Route 3 for 5.6 miles and merge onto BC 93 and 95 to Fort Steele, 4.9 miles to the northeast.

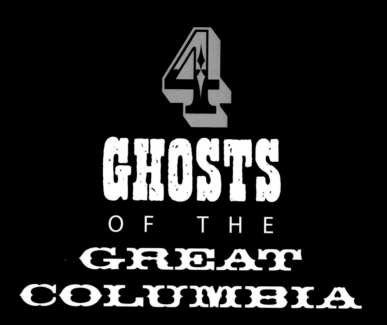

4

GHOSTS

OF THE

GREAT
COLUMBIA

SOUTHWESTERN WASHINGTON IS A DELIGHTFUL PLACE for a vacation, whether for days or weeks. Although many of the ghost towns are of minor importance, the sum of all the sites and sights make the area quite memorable. Two additional attractions are near Astoria, Oregon, across the Columbia River. In fact, crossing the 1966 Astoria–Megler Bridge is an experience in itself.

The Columbia is the lifeblood of southwestern Washington and northwestern Oregon. Most of the towns in the region came into being as a result of the opportunities afforded by the mighty river. The river travels 1,243 miles from Columbia Lake in British Columbia to the Pacific Ocean. When it coursed by Northport, a site in chapter 2, it had already covered slightly more than five hundred miles. By the time it passes Skamokawa, this chapter's opening entry, it is only about thirty-five miles from its destination.

This chapter is arranged for travelers coming from Interstate 5 at Longview and heading west toward the Pacific Ocean. Most of the minor sites, except for three, are right along your route. The closer you get to the ocean, the more interesting the sites become. And, like a good novel, the best ghost town of this chapter is saved for last.

The charming Oysterville, Washington, house of Captain A. T. Stearn dates to 1869.

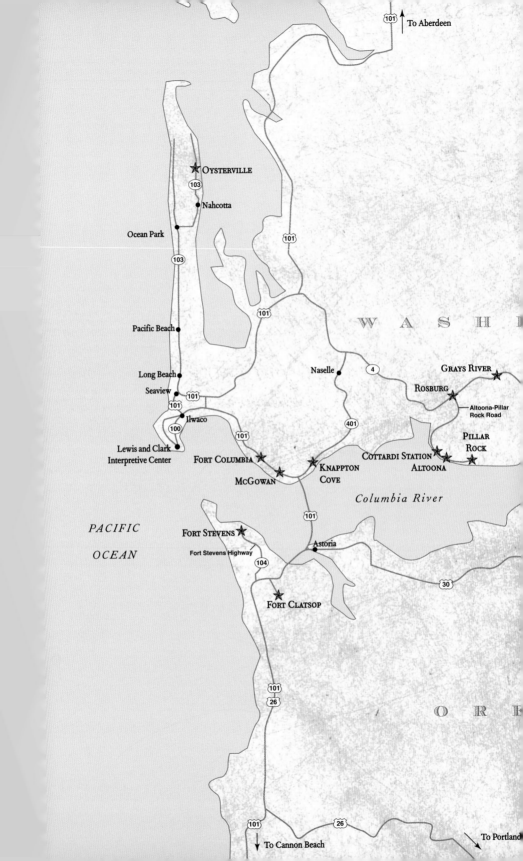

To Aberdeen
101

OYSTERVILLE
103
Nahcotta
Ocean Park
103

W A S H I

Pacific Beach
101

Naselle
4
GRAYS RIVER
Long Beach
ROSBURG
Seaview
101
101
Altoona-Pillar
Rock Road
101
100
Ilwaco
401
PILLAR
ROCK
Lewis and Clark
Interpretive Center
FORT COLUMBIA
COTTARDI STATION
McGowan
KNAPPTON
COVE
ALTOONA

PACIFIC

Columbia River
101

OCEAN
FORT STEVENS
Astoria
Fort Stevens Highway
104
30

FORT CLATSOP

101
26

O R

101
26

To Cannon Beach
To Portland

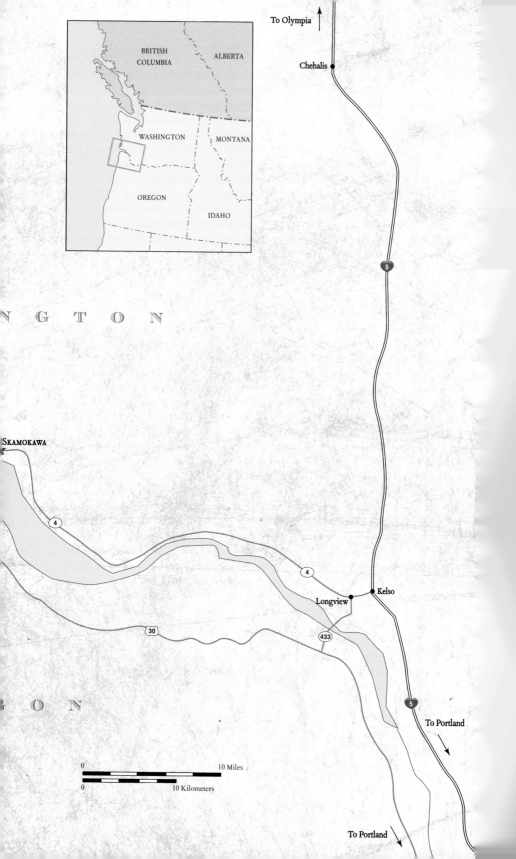

SKAMOKAWA

Skamokawa (skuh-MAHK-uh-way) is, according to residents I talked to, a town on the rebound. An attractive park and campground, beautiful views of the Columbia River, and several historic buildings have made the town a weekend destination.

The settlers who created this small community beginning in the 1860s adopted a name associated with their townsite long before their arrival. *Skamokawa* is a Wahkiakum Indian word meaning "smoke on the water," a reference to the fog that often forms where the river of the same name enters the Columbia.

Migrants from the East Coast of the United States settled the area. Scandinavians followed in the 1870s, because they were attracted by the Columbia's salmon and the coastline's abundant forests. Those industries, along with rich farm and dairy land, brought Skamokawa its peak prosperity in the 1890s. It became a National Historic District in 1976.

DRIVING THROUGH SKAMOKAWA

The town's most obvious attraction sits dramatically on a hill on your right as you enter town: the 1894 schoolhouse, which closed to students in 1926. When the Ocean Beach Highway was constructed through town in the 1930s, the school was moved to its present location and was subsequently purchased by the fraternal organization Order of the Redmen. In 1992 the building, still known as Redmen Hall, opened as the River Life Interpretive Center. It features displays of memorabilia, historic photographs, and audio-visual presentations.

WHEN YOU GO

Skamokawa is 31.6 miles west of Longview on Washington Highway 4. Longview is 564 miles from Fort Steele, the last entry in chapter 3, and 128 miles south of Seattle on Interstate 5.

Skamokawa's 1894 Redmen Hall now houses the River Life Interpretive Center.

GRAYS RIVER AND ROSBURG

The town of Grays River was named for its adjacent river, which was so named because it flows into Grays Bay, on the Columbia. Both honor Captain Robert Gray, who discovered the Columbia in 1792 and named the great river for his ship, the *Columbia Rediviva*.

Rosburg, a couple of miles west of Grays River, was founded in the 1880s by farmers who became weary of rowing to Grays River for mail. They received permission for their own post office, but they had difficulty talking anyone into accepting the post. Finally, a German named Christian Rosberg accepted, although his neighbors had to describe to him in German what his duties entailed. Rosburg, with a slight alteration to the postmaster's name, was born.

WALKING AND DRIVING AROUND GRAYS RIVER

The principal reason for stopping in Grays River is its covered bridge, south of town on a clearly marked historic loop. The 158-foot-long, 14-foot-wide bridge, constructed in 1905, is the last covered bridge still in use on a public road in

Grays River's 1905 covered bridge is the only one of its kind open to public traffic in the state of Washington.

A "Lamb of God" headstone in Rosburg's cemetery shows the effects of years of rain and humidity.

Washington. It was constructed by the H. P. Ahlberg family, according to a sign on the south end of the bridge, and covered in 1906 because their livestock were slipping on the planks. When you drive through the bridge, open your windows and listen to the echoes. It doesn't take too much imagination to hear hoofbeats. On a visit in 2011, I heard a strange chuffing sound coming through the bridge as I was getting my camera ready, and out came a vintage tractor, obviously still in use. That was a genuine step-back-in-time moment.

Grays River Cemetery Road takes you about 0.2 of a mile north from the center of town to the town's graveyard. This well-kept cemetery, located in a mostly cleared area surrounded by forest, contains many graves of Scandinavians.

WALKING AND DRIVING AROUND ROSBURG

The Rosburg Cemetery, adjacent to the Rosburg Store on the south side of the highway, dates from 1885. Many of the graves are for people from Germany and Scandinavia and include such names as Lindberg, Ericson, Andresen, and Olsen. Over in a kind of alcove on the southwest side of the cemetery are some graves of the Anderson family, including a small marker for Baby Augusta, with only one date: 1895.

Across from the Rosburg Store is a road that heads up to the Rosburg School, which is made of brick but has a wooden gymnasium addition.

WHEN YOU GO

Grays River is 11.8 miles northwest of Skamokawa on Washington Highway 4. To reach the covered bridge, look for Loop Road on your left shortly after you have crossed the bridge over Grays River on Washington Highway 4. The road winds down quickly to Covered Bridge Road, where you will turn left to the bridge. There is a parking area on the far (south) end of the bridge. If you miss the first turn onto Loop Road, there's a second turnoff to the left in Grays River, which also features a few aging buildings.

Rosburg is 2.1 miles west of Grays River on Washington Highway 4.

COTTARDI STATION, ALTOONA, AND PILLAR ROCK

A short backroads detour out of Rosburg takes you to three ghost towns that introduce you more intimately to life along the Columbia River. Two more sites later in the chapter will increase the experience. Although all five sites are only minor ghost towns, I recommend them highly, principally for the spectacular views you will enjoy of the mighty Columbia. But before visiting the towns themselves, here's some background on the river's effect on its human inhabitants.

Native Americans had been using the Columbia River for both transportation and fishing long before the arrival of Europeans and Americans. As mentioned in the Grays River entry, Englishman Robert Gray "discovered" and named the Columbia River in 1792, but that had little effect upon the actual use of the river. A more important event, at least as far as the United States was concerned, was the expedition by Meriwether Lewis and William Clark's Corps of Discovery, which utilized the river in their voyage to the Pacific Ocean in 1805. That epic journey greatly increased interest in the Pacific Northwest, especially by fur traders. In 1825, Great Britain's Hudson's Bay Company established a near monopoly in a fur-trading industry that spread throughout the Columbia River area, with furs being brought to Fort Vancouver (a National Historic Site located at Vancouver, on the Washington side of the river, near present-day Portland, Oregon), where they were shipped to England.

Major commercial use of the Columbia River began after gold and silver deposits were found in what would become the states of Idaho and Montana. The Columbia, along with its principal tributary, the Snake River, became the route by which enormous quantities of ore were shipped from Lewiston, Idaho, through the Oregon ports of Portland and Astoria, and then to San Francisco and other markets. The Oregon Steam Navigation Company, chartered in 1860, monopolized the route. In 1861, in a six-month period from June to December, $2.5 million in ore passed through Portland. From 1864 until 1867, a reported $21.4 million in gold and silver was transported. The trade went both ways, as eastbound boats carried supplies for the mining frenzy. And when the rush for gold and silver finally abated, a more permanent kind of "gold" replaced it: golden grain—as eastern Washington and Oregon, as well as Idaho and Montana, became major agricultural suppliers.

Two deteriorating residences still remain from the days when Altoona was a thriving cannery town.

Wharf and building pilings are all that remain of the cannery and the fish receiving station at Cottardi Station and Altoona.

Another commercial bonanza along the Columbia River began in 1866 when brothers William, George, and Robert Hume established the first salmon cannery on the river. The first two brothers had invented a process of packing salmon into tins and originally had plants along the Sacramento River in California, where their younger brother joined them. They moved their operation to the Columbia River when the Sacramento salmon population collapsed. Youngest brother Joseph joined them in Washington, and eventually the four Hume brothers owned half the canneries along the river.

Salmon, long favored by discriminating palates but unavailable at any great distance from river sources, became a staple commodity because of the canning process. In the peak year of 1883, forty canneries were in operation on the Columbia, packing an impressive 634,000 cases that weighed forty-eight pounds each. That output was worth more than $3 million. Eventually more than eighty canneries flourished. Of course, the canneries weren't alone in their success; hundreds of fishermen, with their twenty-five-foot gillnet boats, supplied the canneries with their catch. And this is where the next four ghost towns in this chapter come in.

The scenic road you will be taking to Cottardi Station, Altoona, and Pillar Rock was made possible when a bridge was erected over Grays River in 1931. The road was extended to Cottardi Station in 1935, but it did not reach Altoona, less than a half a mile east, until 1943.

Cottardi Station was named for Baptiste Cottardi, an Italian immigrant who procured a homesteading parcel and built a house at the spot in 1892, the same year he became an American citizen at age fifty-six. He called his homestead

Cottardi Station. Cottardi and his son Amelio earned a living in the summer by salmon fishing with their gillnet boats, and they supplemented their income in the winter by collecting and providing cord wood for the steamboats that navigated the river (and also provided transportation for the family). In 1907, the Columbia River Packers Association (CRPA) purchased the site from the Cottardis and built a receiving and weighing station on pilings on the shoreline for area fishermen to bring in their catch. A warehouse, a fish house, a receiving station, and several residences comprised the site.

Altoona predates Cottardi Station. The aforementioned Hudson's Bay Company used the site as a fish receiving station and saltery in 1830, shipping its product to the Sandwich Islands (now called Hawaii). The saltery was necessary because the Hume brothers had not yet invented and perfected the canning process. So it was only appropriate, perhaps, that in the 1860s William Hume of the cannery business constructed a fish-receiving station at the site of the saltery, which was then called Hume Station. Leif Pulliam ran the station for Hume, but in 1900 Pulliam, a husband and father of four, died a strange and unfortunate death. When his dog jumped into his boat, it tripped both triggers of a double-barreled shotgun—which Pulliam had put in his boat to go duck hunting—and he died shortly after being shot.

After Pulliam's death, Hans and Nellie Petersen, who had previously logged 830 acres in the area, took over the running of Hume Station. They added to the fish receiving station when they built a hotel and saloon at the site. When a post office was granted in 1901, Hans Petersen was the postmaster, and the small town was named, with an extra "o" apparently added by the U.S. Postal Service, for Altona, Germany—Hans's hometown and the name of his fish launch. Eventually, Petersen built a cannery at Altoona, and the Cottardis began selling their catches to Petersen.

By 1910, Hans Petersen's Altoona Packing Company was the fourth largest on the Columbia River. Nevertheless, it failed financially in 1935 and was sold to the Columbia River Packers Association, which, as previously mentioned, already owned Cottardi Station. The CRPA moved its headquarters from Cottardi Station to Altoona, effectively ending the fishing life of Cottardi Station. A fire destroyed most, but not all, of Cottardi Station in 1939, and the Altoona cannery closed in 1947 with the decline of the river's salmon industry.

Amelio Cottardi's residence was one of only two homes to be spared in a fire at Cottardi Station in 1939.

Pillar Rock, a natural formation in the Columbia River near the northern shore, was noted (but not named) by William Clark as the Corps of Discovery neared the Pacific Ocean. In fact, it was only a few miles downstream from Pillar Rock that Clark exclaimed in his journal that the ocean was in view.

The rock itself stood between seventy-five and one hundred feet tall (depending upon the tide) until it was unceremoniously flattened by about fifty feet for the installation of a navigation marker and a light.

Like Altoona, the location of Pillar Rock's cannery was previously used for a saltery owned by the Hudson's Bay Company. But the cannery, called the Pillar Rock Packing Company, preceded Altoona's by almost twenty-five years. It was established in 1877 by John Temple Mason Harrington, a six-foot, three-inch Englishman who weighed 250 pounds and had a ruddy complexion and a bright shock of red hair. He was known throughout the Columbia salmon industry as "the Laird of Pillar Rock." His cannery closed in 1947, the same year as Altoona's. They were the last two of the eighty-one canneries on the river to cease operation. The completion of the Grand Coulee Dam in 1941 led to the eventual demise of the salmon industry on the Columbia.

The Pillar Rock brand, however, survives to this day. The label prominently displays the mighty Pillar Rock (before it was flattened), surrounded by gillnet boats. So the Columbia River and its dramatic rock remain as icons of the salmon industry—for salmon that were caught and canned in Alaska.

DRIVING TO AND WALKING AROUND COTTARDI STATION, ALTOONA, AND PILLAR ROCK

As mentioned earlier in this entry, the main reason to take the Altoona–Pillar Rock Road is the captivating scenery. But you still will have a ghost town adventure.

Cottardi Station consists of at least one occupied residence and one that appears deserted, although it still has its windows. Amelio Cottardi built this house, and the entire Cottardi family moved into it after the sale of Cottardi Station in 1907, a sale that included Baptiste Cottardi's residence. I mentioned earlier the terrible boating-hunting accident that killed Leif Pulliam of Altoona in 1900. A year after that accident, Leif's widow, Dora, married Leif's brother Jim. In 1922, Jim and Dora moved into the house formerly owned by Amelio Cottardi, the empty house standing at the former community today. Pilings from the fish receiving station stand in the river.

Altoona, east of Cottardi Station, features at least two older wooden buildings, one of them collapsing, and a few modern ones. Some buildings are partially hidden in lush overgrowth. Wharf pilings rise above the river, reminding us of the town's former cannery. Altoona, like Cottardi Station, is in a lovely setting, with the dramatic coastline, and, of course, the breadth of the majestic Columbia unfolding before it.

A steep climb out of Altoona takes you into the damp, thick forest that stands along the Columbia. The road proceeds past some modern residences at or near the former communities of Elliott's Landing and Dahlia, and it ends at the townsite of Pillar Rock, which features several occupied homes and the huge cannery (only partially visible from the road). Trespassing is forbidden at the site. Because your view of the cannery is so obstructed, you might choose not to take the road from Altoona to Pillar Rock. The best way to see the cannery would be by boat or plane. Historic photographs of the cannery are available by searching Washington archives on the Internet, and you can get a satellite view of it by using Google maps.

WHEN YOU GO

Altoona–Pillar Rock Road heads south immediately east of the Rosburg Store. Cottardi Station is 6.2 miles south of Rosburg. Altoona is 0.4 of a mile beyond Cottardi Station. Pillar Rock is 3.7 miles east of Altoona.

KNAPPTON COVE

Knappton was settled by and named for Jabez Burrell Knapp, who in 1867 purchased land from which he believed he could produce cement. He constructed a town he named Cementville, only to discover that the prospective quarry wasn't as deep as he hoped. Knapp subsequently opened a sawmill, which proved to be far more lucrative than cement, supplying lumber for canneries and pilings for wharves.

In 1876, Joseph Hume (the youngest of the Hume brothers mentioned in the previous entry) purchased land west of Cementville (later Knappton) and erected a cannery, the Eureka and Epicure Packing Company. By 1899, the cannery had closed and the U.S. government purchased the property to convert it to the Columbia River Quarantine Station. The north shore was chosen at the insistence of Astoria residents, who did not want immigrants with possibly infectious diseases quarantined on their side of the river.

Knappton itself existed into the 1930s, but fire and flooding reduced it to mere pilings. The reason to visit the site is not Knappton, but rather the quarantine station, now the Knappton Cove Heritage Center.

The quarantine station served until 1938 as a kind of Ellis Island of the Columbia River, where thousands of Asians and Europeans were inspected before being allowed to settle in the western United States. After ship fumigation and

The 1912 hospital at Knappton Cove is now part museum, part vacation rental.

personal delousing, those found to be carrying such deadly diseases as cholera, typhus, yellow fever, bubonic plague, or smallpox were quarantined and treated in the 1912 hospital, known as a lazaretto, which now serves as the heritage center museum. The hospital is part museum, part vacation rental. Unfortunately, at this writing, the building is open only during the summer on Saturday from 1 to 4 p.m. or by appointment. Whether open or not, the hospital is well worth a photograph, and historical plaques provide basic information about the quarantine station.

WALKING AROUND KNAPPTON COVE

Today seven buildings make up Knappton Cove, which was added to the National Register of Historic Places in 1980. The structures are on private property, so you should restrict your exploration to the immediate area near the parking lot in front of the hospital, where the plaques are located. If people are occupying the vacation rental, please respect their privacy. I spent the night in the vacation rental and was delighted with the experience.

Immediately to the east of the hospital stands the 1926 combination mess hall and kitchen that accommodated both personnel and patients. A large house close to the highway actually predates the quarantine station. It was the residence of the superintendent of the Eureka and Epicure Packing Company, the earlier salmon cannery.

Across the road from the station today are the rotting pilings of the huge wharves where ships would be docked so inspectors could evaluate the health of those seeking entry into the United States. As a result of this station, the Columbia River area was relatively free of the scourges that once decimated other parts of the world.

WHEN YOU GO

*Knappton Cove is 19.8 miles southwest of Rosburg. From Rosburg, continue northwest on Washington Highway 4 for 11 miles. Turn left on Washington Highway 401 in Naselle. Continue on Highway 401 for 8.8 miles to Knappton Cove. (**Note:** Between mileposts 8 and 9 is a turnoff for Knappton Road. Ignore it, as it does not lead to Knappton Cove.) For more information on the buildings and hours of visitation of Knappton Cove, visit www. knapptoncoveheritagecenter.org.*

FORT CLATSOP

Oregon's wonderful, historic town of Astoria, which had the first U.S. post office west of the Rocky Mountains, features many Victorian homes and other outstanding attractions, including the Astoria Column and the Columbia River Maritime Museum. Two "ghost forts" near Astoria are the focus for this and the following entry.

Meriwether Lewis and William Clark's Corps of Discovery, sent by President Thomas Jefferson to find the most direct route to the Pacific Ocean, left Camp Dubois, near present-day Hartford, Illinois, in May 1804. They saw the Pacific Ocean from the Columbia River in November 1805. The Corps of Discovery spent a cold, miserable month on the north shore of the Columbia, mainly pinned down at a spot Clark dubbed Dismal Nitch (his spelling of *niche*), which is now commemorated by a highway rest stop just east of the Astoria–Megler Bridge.

The first reconstruction of Fort Clatsop, done in 1955, burned in 2005. This second reconstruction, completed in 2006, is more faithful to drawings by Captain William Clark.

On that northern shore, the Corps took a vote whether or not to move to the southern shore, where the friendly Clatsop Indians said there was more game, particularly elk, along with better living conditions. The vote is significant because York, Clark's slave, and Sacagawea, their invaluable guide and interpreter, were both allowed to vote on the decision, held in the far reaches of the American wilderness. This was far ahead of its time: The Fifteenth Amendment to the Constitution, giving former male slaves the right to vote, and the Nineteenth Amendment, allowing women to vote, were, respectively, 65 and 115 years in the future. The band decided to move to the south shore, although Sacagawea voted with the minority.

The felling of trees for what would become Fort Clatsop, named for those Indians, began on December 10, 1805. Of the thirty-three men in the Corps of Discovery, it is estimated that probably no more than a dozen actually constructed the fort, because several men accompanied Clark at the time of the fort's construction to discover a route to the Pacific Ocean from the winter quarters and

others were needed to hunt game to provide sustenance for all. Despite the limited work force, the entire party was ensconced in the fort for the first time on Christmas Day. They spent a wet, cold winter at the fort, with rain or snow occurring on 94 of their 106 days—with only six days of true sunshine. They departed on March 23, 1806.

The Lewis and Clark Expedition took two years, four months, and nine days, which was twice as long as had been expected. They traveled 7,689 miles. Their return to St. Louis was hailed as the remarkable feat that it was because many had feared that the overdue Corps of Discovery members had perished.

In 1811, back near where the Columbia River meets the Pacific, a member of the Astor Party, which was sent to establish a fur trading outpost (now Astoria) at the mouth of the Columbia, went in search of the Lewis and Clark fort and found "piles of rough logs, overgrown with parasite creepers." Two years later, a British party found that the site lay "in total ruins, the wood having been cut down and destroyed by the Indians." In 1901, the Oregon Historical Society purchased three acres that presumably included the site, with plans for a demarcation.

It took more than half a century. In 1955, a reproduction fort, based on William Clark's own drawings, was constructed in time for the sesquicentennial of the building of the original fort. Although no one knows for certain the exact location of the original, it is certain that it was in the immediate vicinity of the reproduction. The site was named the Fort Clatsop Memorial Site in 1959. The reconstruction became a national favorite of schoolchildren, tourists, archaeologists, and scholars. In October 2005, however, mere weeks prior to the bicentennial celebration of the construction of Lewis and Clark's fort, a fire in one of the structure's open-pit fireplaces apparently ignited floorboards with dry rot. The fort was destroyed.

A new reconstruction was dedicated in December 2006, fourteen months after the fire. It is more faithful to the original fort than the 1955 effort, because fifty years of additional research established several probable inaccuracies. In addition, using modern tools like saws (which were used in the first reconstruction) was avoided whenever possible. About seven hundred people assisted in the second reconstruction, which took more than a year, compared to something like a dozen men finishing the original in slightly more than two weeks. But as Pete Field, project manager of the later reconstruction reminds us, "Remember, their fort only had to last three months—we want this one to last fifty or more years."

WALKING AROUND FORT CLATSOP

Please allow yourself at least a couple of hours to explore Fort Clatsop. You will be standing, after all, in one of the oldest historic American places in the entire West. Take plenty of time to walk around the visitors' center, which includes videos, extraordinary displays, and a remarkable sculpture of the principals of the Corps of Discovery, including Seaman, Meriwether Lewis's faithful, heroic, and massive Newfoundland dog, who completed the entire journey.

Immediately inside the main gate of Fort Clatsop are the small parade grounds. Visible on the left are three separate rooms that served as soldiers' quarters.

You can also hike extensively in the area, including a thirteen-mile round-trip walk from the park to the Pacific Ocean, following a route similar to one the explorers took.

But the star attraction is the fort itself. You will meet park employees, who are dressed in period outfits, answering questions and demonstrating skills that were necessary to survive the cold, wet winter of 1805–1806. Many of those skills are hands-on activities, geared especially for children. Want to try to write with a quill pen?

To learn even more about the explorers and their expedition, visit the Lewis and Clark Interpretive Center near Ilwaco, Washington (see page 128).

WHEN YOU GO

From Knappton Cove, continue 3.1 miles on Washington Highway 401 to the Astoria-Megler Bridge and cross the Columbia into Oregon.

Before you reach the bridge, you will pass the Dismal Nitch Rest Area, near the spot where Lewis and Clark's Corps of Discovery camped in great discomfort (hence the name) in November 1805.

From Astoria, go south on U.S. Highway 101. At 4 miles from downtown Astoria is a turnoff to Fort Stevens, but do not take it. Continue on U.S. 101 for another 0.5 of a mile and turn left at the marked turn for Fort Clatsop. Follow the clearly marked route for 3.1 miles.

FORT STEVENS

Fort Stevens is a fort of the nineteenth and twentieth centuries, unlike Fort Clatsop. But if you enjoyed Forts Flagler, Worden, and Casey, which are featured in chapter 1, you will also appreciate Fort Stevens (and Fort Columbia, featured later in this chapter).

Fort Stevens was constructed during the Civil War and named for General Isaac Ingalls Stevens, who died early in that same war. Along with Forts Columbia and Camby in Washington, Fort Stevens was part of the three-fort defense system that guarded the Pacific Coast and mouth of the Columbia River, initially from potential British threats during regional tensions over border disputes until 1870, and later during World Wars I and II.

In the latter war, Fort Stevens actually came under attack on June 21 and 22, 1942, when a Japanese submarine fired seventeen shells at the fort, damaging only a baseball field's backstop.

Following the fort's decommission shortly after World War II, the structures of Fort Stevens were sold at auction and the armaments were scrapped. Although the fort is very incomplete, several historic attractions remain—now as Fort Stevens State Park and Fort Stevens Historical Site—to remind us of its years of service to the United States.

Homes on officers' row are now privately owned and are not part of the Fort Stevens Historical Site.

WALKING AND DRIVING AROUND FORT STEVENS

At Fort Stevens today, you can explore enormous gun batteries, take a tour on a World War II army truck, and examine foundations of soldiers' barracks. A military museum, housed in the 1911 War Games Building, features an excellent model of the fort showing how it looked during World War II. In addition, you will receive a brochure that suggests walking and driving tours.

Be sure to visit three attractions that are a short distance away from the main fort, only two of which are shown on the brochure's map. The first is the 1910 to 1912 brick guardhouse, which is listed on the National Register of Historic Places. It is often open for tours with volunteer docents. South of the guardhouse on Russell Drive (but not on your map) is officers' row, where you can photograph lovely two-story wood-frame houses that are now private homes and are no longer part of the fort or the park.

The imposing brick guardhouse at Fort Stevens is occasionally open for tours.

A miscreant mannequin inmate stands inside an eight-bed cell at Fort Stevens.

Beyond officers' row on Russell Drive is the picturesque military cemetery, established in 1868. The pavement will end before you arrive at the graveyard, but keep going until you reach it. The earliest burial is for Private August Stahlberger, who drowned in the Columbia River while "under the influence."

WHEN YOU GO

From Fort Clatsop, return to U.S. Highway 101. Instead of turning onto the highway, cross it and proceed 1.3 miles to Warrenton. Continue through Warrenton 2.9 miles to Hammond. Fort Stevens is immediately beyond Hammond.

McGOWAN

McGowan, Washington, was named for Patrick J. McGowan, who in 1853 purchased 320 acres of a Catholic mission land grant and built a salmon-packing plant. In 1904 he donated land for St. Mary's Catholic Church. I find it interesting that it took him fifty-one years to make that donation. Was he near death, perhaps?

DRIVING THROUGH McGOWAN

That church, a clapboard building sitting on a cut-stone foundation, is the only historic building left standing at McGowan. Unlike the earlier canning-factory sites in this chapter (Altoona, Pillar Rock, and Knappton), no pilings of wharves or piers still exist at McGowan.

When you cross the Astoria–Megler Bridge back into Washington, you enter the territory of the Ilwaco Railroad & Steam Navigation Company, popularly known as the Clamshell Railway. The railroad, which operated from 1888 until 1930, began in Megler, a now-vanished community that was an important ferry port across from Astoria prior to the completion of the Astoria–Megler Bridge. The tracks ran for twenty-seven miles up the North Beach Peninsula to Nahcotta. McGowan was the first stop along the route, followed by Fort Columbia.

The town of Megler, incidentally, was apparently originally called Chinookville but was renamed in honor of Joseph D. Megler, a German-born tinsmith from New York who practiced his trade in the salmon industry. Joseph Megler represented Wahkiakum County in either the state house or senate for twenty-two years. Pilings and evidence of the ferry landing are all that remain of the community.

WHEN YOU GO

From Fort Stevens, return to Astoria and cross the Astoria–Megler Bridge back into Washington. McGowan is 1.7 miles west of the Astoria–Megler Bridge on U.S. Highway 101.

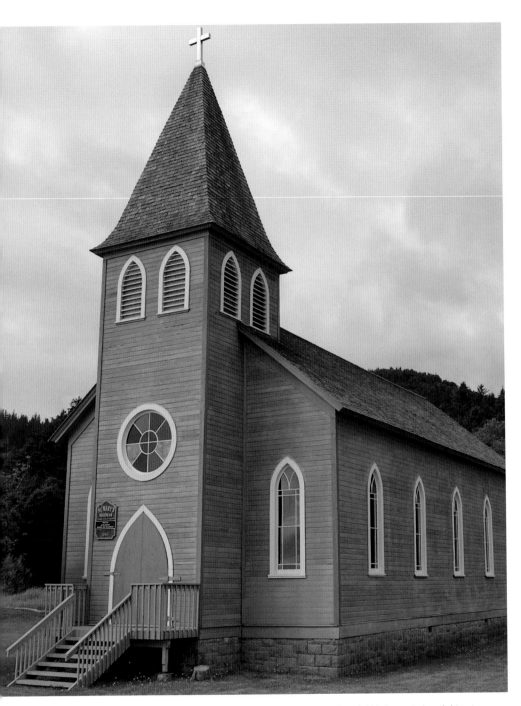

St. Mary's Catholic Church, built in 1904 on land donated by cannery owner Patrick J. McGowan, is the only historic building at the townsite.

FORT COLUMBIA

Along with Fort Canby to the northwest and Fort Stevens to the southwest, Fort Columbia protected the mouth of the Columbia River. Fort Columbia was constructed between 1896 and 1904, more than thirty years after its sister forts, and a close look at a map explains why: It is much farther east than Forts Stevens and Canby, with an unobstructed view of the mouth of the Columbia. It appears that if an enemy ship somehow managed to elude the fire of those two forts, it would be directly in the gun sights of Fort Columbia. These protective fortifications were so imposing that the three-fort harbor defense system never fired a wartime shot.

When Fort Columbia was constructed, the Ilwaco Railroad & Steam Navigation Company (mentioned in the previous entry, McGowan) had been in operation for six years, and a tunnel extended right beneath the proposed location of the fort. The solution was simple: Build the fort on the hill and leave the tunnel intact. Imagine the Pentagon allowing such an arrangement today!

Fort Columbia includes, among other buildings, from right to left, the commanding officer's quarters, the commissioned officers' quarters, the administration building, and the barracks.

The ghostly ruin of the Searchlight Powerhouse stands near another ruin, the New Mine Casemate at Fort Columbia.

Fort Columbia functioned, in some ways, more like a town than a military installation. It had its own firehouse, hospital, theater, and electrical power generating plant. In addition to being soldiers, the men also had more rudimentary duties as bakers, barbers, and even musicians. They worked their own vegetable gardens and had chickens and a dairy cow. For recreation, there was a fort baseball team that competed against nearby towns and even weekend dances were held—with local girls trucked to the fort.

Like Forts Stevens and Canby, Fort Columbia was declared surplus after World War II. It was decommissioned in 1947 and is now part of the Washington state park system.

WALKING AND DRIVING AROUND FORT COLUMBIA

Twelve historic wood-frame buildings, restored to their 1902 appearances, and four coastal defense batteries still stand on the premises of Fort Columbia, making it far more complete than either Fort Stevens (mentioned earlier in this chapter) or Fort Canby (which is, essentially, now a large campground).

Your tour of Fort Columbia begins at the Barracks Interpretive Center. On the first floor are military displays, the mess hall set for a formal occasion, and the kitchen with its massive coal-fired stoves, its sinks, and an oak refrigerator. On the same floor, a viewing room shows a repeating video about the fort. The second floor contains a squad room with beds, lockers, and footlockers still in place; a barbershop; and a large room with displays about the Chinook Indians.

The commanding officer's quarters stand three buildings southeast of the barracks. The lovely home, like the one at Fort Worden featured in chapter 1, has been authentically restored with period furniture and household items. When there are sufficient volunteers, it is open for tours.

As far as the actual armaments are concerned, the original gun batteries were removed after World War II, but two six-inch cannons were brought from Canada and installed in Battery 246 in 1994. They are two of only six such guns remaining in the world.

Two buildings, the Scarborough House (the former hospital) and the Hospital Steward's House, are available as vacation rentals.

The most ghostly building I saw at Fort Columbia hides in the brush on your right not long after you enter the state park and before you climb the hill to the principal attractions. It is the ruin of the Searchlight Powerhouse.

WHEN YOU GO

Fort Columbia is 0.8 of a mile northwest of McGowan on U.S. Highway 101. The entrance to the park is immediately after a tunnel, originally built for the Clamshell Railway and now used for U.S. 101.

THE LEWIS AND CLARK INTERPRETIVE CENTER AND THE NORTH HEAD LIGHTHOUSE

As you travel from Fort Columbia to Oysterville, you should consider visiting the Lewis and Clark Interpretive Center and the North Head Lighthouse, both near Ilwaco.

A tour of the Lewis and Clark Interpretive Center is appropriate either before or after a visit to Fort Clatsop (see page 116). The center is set up so that you encounter Lewis and Clark's journey chronologically as you wind around within the building. You might also enjoy walking around, through, and even beneath the grounds, because the Interpretive Center sits on a "ghost fort," the remnants of the Battery Harvey Allen of Fort Canby. Fort Canby itself is now a large campground but does not feature the historic attractions of the other forts in this book.

The North Head Lighthouse, built in 1898, helped guide mariners away from the shore and toward the mouth of the Columbia River.

The elegant lighthouse keeper's residence, left, and the duplex for his assistants, are now available as vacation rentals at the North Head Lighthouse.

Lighthouses, like old forts, attract people who are interested in ghost towns. You can observe, but not visit, the Cape Disappointment Lighthouse by taking a 1.5-mile round-trip hike on a trail that begins at the interpretive center parking lot. It is also visible from a distance from North Jetty Drive inside Fort Canby State Park.

The North Head Lighthouse, however, is open to the public. From the Interpretive Center, drive north on Washington Highway 100 for about a mile. The turn to the lighthouse is clearly marked. The 1898 building sits, as most of the Pacific Coast's lighthouses do, on a scenic promontory. When you return to the parking lot, take the alternate way back—the original lightkeeper's way. The walkway takes you past the two 1898 lighthouse keepers' residences, which are available as vacation rentals. The western building was for the lightkeeper and his family. The one to the east is a duplex that was for his two assistants and their families.

The Lewis and Clark Interpretive Center is 2 miles southwest of Ilwaco on Washington Highway 100. Ilwaco is 8.8 miles northwest of Fort Columbia.

OYSTERVILLE

Oysterville, a small village near the north end of Long Beach Peninsula, is the ghost town highlight of southwestern Washington. Placed on the National Register of Historic Places in 1976, the charming community offers several carefully tended old residences, a school, a church, a delightful store, and a well-kept historic cemetery.

Oysterville was settled in 1854 by Isaac Alonzo Clark and R. H. Espy, who wanted to harvest and sell oysters from the abundant oyster beds in Shoalwater Bay, now called Willapa Bay. Oysterville became the seat of Pacific County in 1855 and could boast of a newspaper (the *Pacific Journal*), three hotels, a baseball park, a restaurant, a blacksmith shop, three saloons, four general stores, and a cannery. Oysters were shipped to many locations, but the best customers were the restaurants of San Francisco, which was then enjoying the prosperity of the Gold Rush.

Oysterville's 1892 church features an unusual placement of its steeple: It is integrated into both parts of the L-shaped building.

The simple, unadorned interior of Oysterville's Church contains a piano (left), a wood-burning stove, and an organ.

Oysterville's decline began when the Clamshell Railway, constructed from Megler in 1888, ended at Nahcotta, leaving Oysterville isolated at the north end of the peninsula. The oyster beds gave out due to overharvesting in the 1890s, and in 1893 the Pacific County seat was lost to rival South Bend (which features a wonderful 1910 courthouse that is on the National Register of Historic Places). After that, Oysterville began its slide toward the somnolent—but lovely—town it is today.

WALKING AND DRIVING AROUND OYSTERVILLE

A good place to leave your car for a walk around town is the parking lot of the 1907 school, in the center of town on School Road. The shingle-sided wooden building presently serves as a community center.

The most prominent structure in Oysterville, its church, is southeast of the school parking lot. Built in 1892, the church was donated by town cofounder R. H. Espy. Originally a Baptist congregation, the church is now nondenominational. It is very plainly but pleasantly adorned and includes a small side room for overflow attendance. You can obtain a walking-tour brochure of the town in the church's foyer.

Since that handout is detailed and informative, I will only mention three favorite residences of mine. The first, two doors south of the church, is a small red cottage that is the oldest surviving residence in Oysterville, dating from about 1863.

North of the church on the east side of Territory Road is the 1871 R. H. Espy residence. You have to walk east to see its front, as it faces Willapa Bay.

Northeast of the Espy home, on Main Street north of Oysterville Road, stands the small but attractive home, built in 1869, of Captain A. T. Stearn.

Captain A. T. Stearn, noted on a sign as a local hero, lived in this lovely, modest home in Oysterville.

From the intersection of Territory and Oysterville Roads, drive west for 0.2 of a mile to the likeable Oysterville General Store, built in 1919. The store's post office is reportedly the oldest in the state operating under the same name.

Drive west beyond the general store only 0.1 of a mile and turn south into the entrance of the lovely, peaceful Oysterville Cemetery. Immediately inside the gate is the grave of Chief Nahcati (1826–1864), who guided town founders Espy and Clark to the oyster beds of Shoalwater Bay. On all four of my visits, the grave was adorned with seashells left by people paying their respects.

More than a dozen of the graves in the northeast corner of the cemetery are for members of the pioneer Espy family, including Oysterville cofounder Robert Espy (1826–1918) and his wife Julia (1852–1901). The other founder of Oysterville, Isaac A. Clark (1828–1926), is also interred in the graveyard.

Two of the most touching stones are identical side-by-side markers about twenty-five yards south of the Espy graves:

Our Friend
Julius Mack
Drowned in Shoalwater Bay
January 1, 1873
Age 45 years

Our Father
Carl A. Tanger
Drowned in Shoalwater Bay
January 1, 1873
Age 44 years

Oysterville's cofounder, Robert Espy, built this stately residence in 1871. It faces east, looking out to Willapa Bay (formerly Shoalwater Bay).

Mack and Tanger had left a load of lumber out on their boat on Shoalwater Bay on the previous day and went out on New Year's Day morning to retrieve it, with Tanger telling his wife to "wait breakfast." The boat swamped; neither man could swim.

WHEN YOU GO

From Fort Columbia, drive north for less than 2 miles on U.S. Highway 101 to Chinook. Continue on that highway for about 4.5 miles until it divides. I suggest turning left to proceed into Ilwaco, 8.2 miles from Fort Columbia, to visit the extremely interesting Lewis and Clark Interpretive Center (see sidebar on page 128), which is 3 miles southwest of Ilwaco on Washington Highway 100. Then return to Ilwaco and head north on Highway 101 to Seaview, a distance of 2 miles. Just before entering Seaview, Highway 101 turns east, but do not follow it. Instead, continue north on Washington Highway 103 for 15.8 miles through Seaview, Long Beach, Ocean Park, and Nahcotta. When in Nahcotta, be sure to stop to read the humorous sign on the north side of the former Nahcotta post office and store—at this writing Bailey's Bakery and Café—referring to the Ilwaco Railroad. Proceed 3.2 miles north from Nahcotta and turn right at the Oysterville sign on Territory Road. If, on your return trip, you would like to avoid the weekend crawl of traffic along Washington Highway 103 (especially through Long Beach), do what the locals do: When the highway veers right south of Nahcotta, take a left on Sandridge Road, which parallels the highway but avoids all the towns.

5
GHOSTS
OF THE
OREGON
PLAINS

AS CHAPTER 2 DID IN WASHINGTON, this chapter takes you into an Oregon far away from the most popular (and populous) areas of the state. The journey proceeds as a logical trip from Portland, starting with the westernmost towns and ending up with the southernmost site. On the route are several minor ghost towns, along with two of the best in the state—Shaniko and Hardman. The route also offers a natural tie-in with chapter 6, which takes you even farther along Oregon's wonderful back roads.

An abandoned church in Grass Valley, Oregon, needs protection and restoration if it is to survive. The off-center steeple on the church's south side is partially concealed by trees.

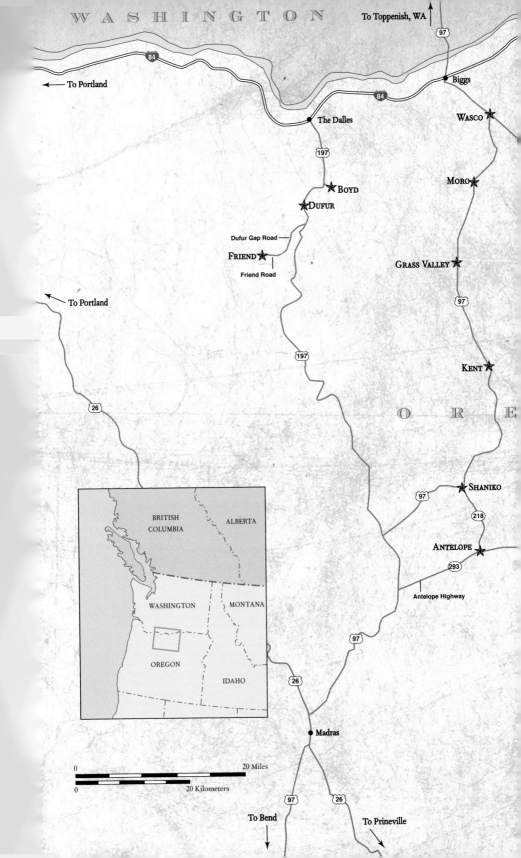

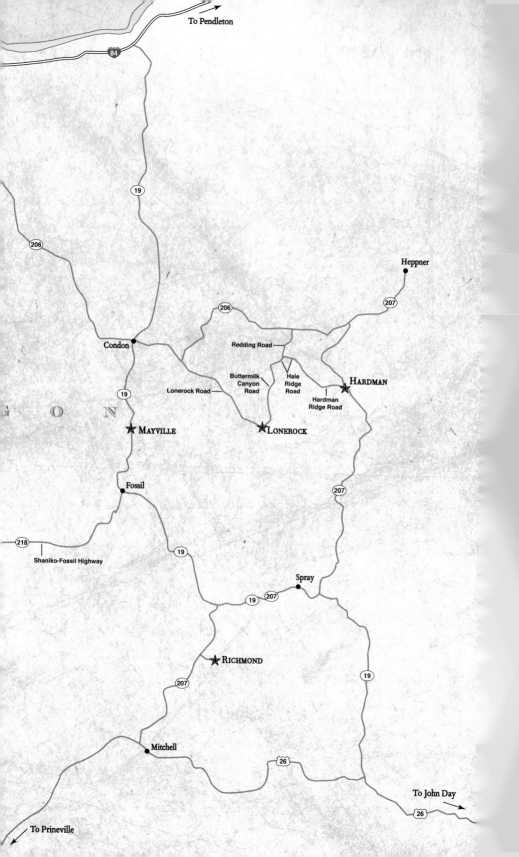

BOYD, DUFUR, AND FRIEND

Boyd and Friend are minor ghost towns worth visiting if you don't mind a limited selection of historic buildings. Between these two genuine ghosts, Dufur is a pleasant, living town that features several attractive structures.

Boyd was settled around 1870 where a small store was erected at an easy crossing of Fifteenmile Creek. The town, which received its post office in 1884, was named in honor of T. P. Boyd, who had built a granary and mill the previous year. The mill was utilized by local wheat farmers, who shipped their flour on to Dufur and The Dalles, first by wagon and then, beginning in 1905, by the recently completed Great Southern Railroad. Boyd's decline was sealed when the tracks were taken up in 1936. The town's post office held on until the 1960s.

DRIVING THROUGH BOYD

Boyd today is a small community with one vacant residence among a few occupied ones. On the south end of town are two historic buildings: T. P. Boyd's large wooden granary and mill sit picturesquely near Fifteenmile Creek, and, behind it stands a wooden structure with a cupola.

Between Boyd and Dufur is the Star No. 23 Rebekah Lodge Community Cemetery. This graveyard is worth a quick detour.

Ranchers first came to the Dufur area in 1852. In 1863, David Imbler built the Fifteenmile Inn along Fifteenmile Creek as a way station for travelers to and from the Cascade Range. The route evolved into a stage and freight route between The Dalles, which is, appropriately enough, about fifteen miles to the north, and Wapinitia, about thirty miles south.

The town that grew along Fifteenmile Creek was named for Andrew J. Dufur, who with his brother Enoch bought acreage here in 1872. The name seems the only fair choice, for the town was actually located on the Dufurs' land. The post office was established in that name in 1878. The Great Southern Railroad came to Dufur in 1905, allowing cheaper transportation of goods north to The Dalles and from there to national markets. Although it is now a wheat-growing area, Dufur was once the site of the country's largest dry-land apple orchard.

T. P. Boyd's wooden grain mill is located along Fifteenmile Creek in Boyd.

WALKING AND DRIVING AROUND DUFUR

In addition to its well-kept residences and an interesting downtown, Dufur today has three special buildings worth examining. The first, located slightly south of the central business district, is the Schreiber House, a large, two-story log cabin at the Dufur Historical Society Living History Museum. The cabin, built in 1900, originally stood in Friend, your next destination.

The Schreiber House, originally located in Friend, is now a part of the Dufur Historical Society Living History Museum.

Behind the Schreiber House stands the Endersby School, moved to this location from Endersby, northwest of Dufur. The school has seven tall windows on its south-facing side, but none on the other three. The windows likely faced east when the building was in Endersby, away from the prominent westerly winds that often assault the Oregon prairie.

The 1907 Balch Hotel, located south of the living history museum across Fifteenmile Creek, is a stately three-story brick structure with beautiful brick patterns on the front. It is on the National Register of Historic Places.

The town of Friend, southwest of Dufur, was named for homesteader George J. Friend and received its post office in 1903. It became the terminus of the Great Southern Railroad when tracks were extended from Dufur in 1913. For a time it prospered as a shipping center for area farmers, sheepherders, ranchers, and loggers. Like Boyd and Dufur, its heyday was over by 1936, when the tracks of the Great Southern were taken up.

WALKING AND DRIVING AROUND FRIEND

The first building of note as you enter Friend from the east is the former general store, just north of a metal silo. The railroad right-of-way runs near the southern end of the building.

The Endersby School, erected in 1894, now stands in Dufur as part of that town's living history museum.

The 1907 Balch Hotel is south of central Dufur across Fifteenmile Creek.

Friend's general store is now on private property, but, at this writing, the property was not posted against trespassing.

A concrete and stone vault is all that still remains of Travis Murrey's mercantile in Friend. Mount Hood forms the dramatic backdrop.

If you return to Friend Road and drive less than 0.2 of a mile west, you will come to Heberlein Road. North of that junction on the west side is a concrete-and-stone vault, the only remnant of Travis Murrey's mercantile.

The 1909 one-room Friend School is 0.3 of a mile west of the Heberlein Road junction. The school, which still serves as a community center, has lost its bell, but it does have a flagpole and two outhouses, labeled "Ladies" and "Gents."

The Friend Cemetery is 0.5 of a mile south of the school. The graveyard sits hidden in trees adjacent to posted private property on the west side of the road.

WHEN YOU GO

Boyd is 11.8 miles southeast of The Dalles, which is 84 miles east of Portland on Interstate 84. Take Exit 87 off I-84 east of The Dalles and head south to U.S. Highway 197. Follow that highway south for 8.6 miles, where a sign points you to Boyd, 0.7 of a mile east.

To reach the Star No. 23 Rebekah Lodge Community Cemetery, return to U.S. 197 and head south. In 1.4 miles, take a right turn and follow the road to the graveyard.

When you leave the cemetery, turn south on U.S. 197 and proceed 1.3 miles to the turnoff of Dufur.

To get to Friend, head south on Dufur's Main Street across Fifteenmile Creek past the Balch Hotel. In 0.3 of a mile, follow the left fork in the road. In 0.6 of a mile you will meet up with U.S. 197. Take that highway south for 1.8 miles, and turn right onto Dufur Gap Road, which has a signpost to Friend. In 4.5 miles, just past Tygh Ridge Road on your left, turn right onto Friend Road. The town of Friend is 5 miles west.

WASCO, MORO, AND GRASS VALLEY

Wasco, Moro, and Grass Valley are living communities north of the ghost towns of Shaniko and Kent. Each features a notable building or two, although they are not nearly as "ghostly" as their neighbors to the south.

Wasco is a tiny town, but the name once meant something very big. Wasco County, named for a local Native American tribe, was formed in 1854 and in its original configuration was the largest county ever in the United States. It extended easterly from the crest of the Cascades across central and eastern Oregon, south to the present Oregon-California border, across the entirety of southern Idaho below the forty-sixth parallel, and to the Continental Divide in western Wyoming, including what is now Grand Teton National Park and Jackson Hole. You really must look at a map to comprehend the size of early Wasco County.

Wasco the town was named for its home county. It is now the largest community in sparsely populated Sherman County. Wasco became the first stop south

The boarded-up Crosfield General Merchandise is located in downtown Wasco.

Wasco has the only complete depot of the once-prosperous Columbia Southern Railroad.

along the Columbia Southern Railroad, which at the turn of the twentieth century became the lifeline for five towns in this chapter: Wasco, Moro, Grass Valley, Kent, and Shaniko. The railroad was intended to stretch from the Columbia River at Biggs Junction (now Biggs) south to Prineville and beyond. It only made it to Shaniko.

WALKING AND DRIVING AROUND WASCO

Wasco today features the only standing, complete depot along the Columbia Southern. The two-story clapboard structure, on the National Register of Historic Places, sits at the south end of downtown. The depot signboard says that Biggs is 9.6 miles north, while Shaniko is 60.2 miles away. Since Shaniko is only about forty-six miles by car, where did the extra miles come from? The answer is that the Columbia Southern did not go south from Wasco, but rather east through the now-vanished town of Klondike and then south through Hay Canyon, after which it headed west back toward Moro.

On the southwest corner of Clark and Barnett Streets stands the 1889 two-story clapboard Oskaloosa Hotel. Several brick commercial buildings also line Clark. East of Clark on Barnett stands the town's elementary school, a solid two-story white building trimmed in gray.

A short side trip from Wasco will take you to the spectral 1895 Locust Grove United Brethren Church, which is located 4.5 miles west of Wasco on Oregon Highway 206. According to a sign affixed to it, the church was last used for a funeral in 1914.

The now-vanished town of Locust Grove, west of Wasco, has only this vacant 1895 United Brethren Church to remind us that a small community once existed here.

A local resident of Grass Valley told me that the abandoned school in Grass Valley was once used, in recent years, by someone growing marijuana, giving a new meaning to "Grass" Valley. The scheme was discovered when utility use at the supposedly empty school was suspiciously high.

WALKING AND DRIVING AROUND MORO

The principal reason to stop at Moro, the seat of Sherman County, is the excellent Sherman County Historical Museum (open daily from May to October), one of the finest regional museums I have visited. The three-building compound features displays beginning with the history of Native Americans, continuing through the Oregon Trail pioneers, and concluding with the wheat farmers who have made central Oregon the producer of 10 percent of the nation's wheat.

While in Moro, you also might wish to photograph the two-story brick Sherman County Courthouse. Constructed in 1899, it is located at Court and Fourth Streets, on the west side of town. Another building worth seeking out is southeast of the courthouse: the 1917 school, on Scott Street.

The Grass Valley Cemetery, including this IOOF section, is north of town.

An array of farm trucks dating from the 1920s to the 1940s—and one lone Jeep—pose for the camera in Grass Valley. (The Jeep is fifth from the left with a spare wheel in front of its grille.)

WALKING AND DRIVING AROUND GRASS VALLEY

Grass Valley, named for the bunch grass that filled the surrounding prairie before the town became an agricultural center, is home to one of the prettiest churches in Oregon. Located south of the center of town and one block west, it features an offset belfry, brick chimney, and Gothic windows. It is also one of the churches in greatest peril. Partially hidden by overgrowth, the church badly needs protection and restoration. To see how it might have once looked, visit the church in Antelope, discussed later in the chapter.

On a hill west of the church is a huge school that closed to students in the mid-1960s. It is a disaster of design, looking as if it were created by someone more accustomed to building structures of great bulk, like grain elevators.

North of town, the small Grass Valley Cemetery provides a stunning view of

Mount Hood to the west as well as fine vistas of Mount Jefferson to the southwest and Washington's Mount Adams to the northwest. The cemetery itself has several infant graves, each with a "Lamb of God" headstone common for graves of the young.

WHEN YOU GO

These three sites are south of Biggs, which is 20 miles east of The Dalles on Interstate 84. Drive 8.5 miles south on U.S. Highway 97 to a junction with Oregon Highway 206. Follow Highway 206 east for 0.9 of a mile to Wasco. Moro is 10 miles south of Wasco on U.S. 97. Grass Valley is 9.5 miles south of Moro on that same highway, and its cemetery is 1 mile north of town on U.S. 97, after a turnoff to the west.

KENT

With its two grain elevators standing like sentinels of the prairie, Kent is visible from miles away. The town was settled in the 1880s, receiving its post office in 1887. Its name reportedly was drawn out of a hat, submitted by a citizen who thought it was "nice and short." The Columbia Southern Railroad laid tracks to Kent in 1899, and for a short time the town boomed as the terminus of that railroad. When the tracks were extended to Shaniko, however, Kent declined, although it remained significant for its grain elevators, from which stored wheat was shipped north by rail to Biggs Junction. When the tracks were washed out in 1964, Kent, along with Shaniko, headed toward becoming a ghost town.

WALKING AND DRIVING AROUND KENT

One indicator of a genuine ghost town might be that the highway speed limit sign as you enter town does not even require that you slow down. But slowing down for Kent—and stopping for a visit—is exactly what you should do.

A former gas station and café on the north end of Kent attests to the fact that plastic deteriorates less quickly than wood, paint, and shake shingles.

Phillips 66 gasoline sold for 66 ½ cents per gallon when this gas station and café closed in Kent.

Kent today has several historic buildings. On the north end of town stands an empty combination café and gas station (possible motto: "Eat Here, Get Gas"?) advertising petrol at the bargain price of 66½ cents per gallon.

Immediately across the street from the service station is a beehive stone structure with a metal cap. It was built in the 1930s to house a generator that produced electric power to the gas station and to the station owner's home, which stood west of the generator.

Kent's combination gymnasium and auditorium is one block east of the service station. A large, extraordinarily plain school built in 1902 that once stood north of the gym is now merely a concrete foundation, having burned in the mid-1980s after about twenty years of disuse. Its near twin still stands in Grass Valley, which you passed through on your way south toward Kent. The gymnasium, on my third visit in 2002, was still in informal use: Despite the deteriorating roof, the wooden court was still playable, and one basketball rim had a net. A fully inflated basketball rested on the court, and, as a former high school basketball coach, I took advantage of the opportunity. When I returned in 2010, the gym was completely boarded up, and I was denied my chance to shoot more jump shots.

An odd, beehive-shaped concrete and stone structure, across the street from the gas station and café in Kent, once housed a generator that gave power to the station across the street and to the residence of the station's owner's house.

South of the gymnasium stand those dramatic grain elevators, one made of concrete and the other of wood. The six-story-tall wooden grain elevator, made of two-by-six-inch boards laid flat, is especially eye-catching.

Several other wooden buildings can be found on Dobie Point Road leading to the elevators. One of these buildings once had an exterior staircase to the Independent Order of Odd Fellows (IOOF) Hall on the second floor. Across the street are two wooden false-front buildings. When I first photographed them in 1982, one of them had a sign proclaiming it to be the Smith Store, selling "hardware, groceries, and implements." The sign has since completely faded and is now illegible.

A sign over the cemetery north of town declares it to be the Kent Cemetery, but a U.S. Geological Survey topographic map indicates that it was previously known as the Odd Fellows Cemetery. Whatever the name, the northwest section of the graveyard features a touching, personalized grave

Two dilapidated false-front commercial buildings stand along Dobie Point Road in Kent.

for Jerry M. Wilson III, who died in 1948 at age four. The concrete slab that covers his grave has glass insulators embedded around the perimeter, and two of his toys, a cap pistol and a metal airplane, are embedded within the slab. The boy's nickname, "Skippy," is spelled out with small stones, and a large lilac bush grows at the foot of the grave.

WHEN YOU GO

Kent is 12.8 miles south of Grass Valley on U.S. Highway 97. The town's cemetery is just west of the highway 1.4 miles north of town, so if you are coming from Grass Valley, you will arrive at the cemetery before reaching the town.

SHANIKO

For about a decade, Shaniko could boast that it was the largest wool-shipping center in the world. The town came into being in 1900 as an important stop on the route of the Columbia Southern Railroad. It turned out to be the railroad's southern terminus. Serving as the center of commerce for a 20,000-square-mile area of central Oregon, Shaniko was the place where ranchers and farmers took sheep, wool, cattle, and wheat to market.

The town's name comes from a Native American mispronunciation of the last name of August Schernechau, who owned a stage stop at nearby Cross Hollows, south of present-day Shaniko. When the railroad came to Shaniko, virtually everything in Cross Hollows was moved to the newer community. By 1900, Shaniko had a population of 172, most of them construction workers building themselves a town.

In the banner year of 1903, more than 1.1 million bushels of wheat were sold, and wool sales in excess of $3 million made Shaniko the "Wool Capital of the World." Wool sales are believed to have topped $5 million in 1904.

Shaniko's beautifully restored hotel, erected around 1900, stands empty and for sale at this writing.

The decline of Shaniko began in 1911, when a competing railroad, the Oregon Trunk, was completed along the Deschutes River to Bend, which then linked central Oregon south to California markets. Shaniko was merely the terminus of a dead-end railroad. A fire that same year consumed many downtown buildings, which were never rebuilt.

The demand for Oregon wool declined after World War I as Australia and New Zealand began producing less expensive wool, further reducing Shaniko's importance. The town's reduction to ghost town status was assured by 1942, when the railroad tracks were taken up to Kent. The town's progress was also slowed by the fact that it did not have electricity until the mid-1940s.

Incidentally, the town is located virtually on the forty-fifth parallel, making it equidistant between the North Pole and the equator.

WALKING AROUND SHANIKO

The Shaniko Hotel has always been the anchor of Shaniko. Built around 1900 as the Columbia Southern Hotel, the two-story brick edifice has not only offered pleasant lodgings, but it also has had a very good restaurant and a gift shop. Unfortunately, the hotel is closed and up for sale at this writing—reportedly at a highly inflated price, so that it is only nominally for sale. I visited at length with a longtime resident of Shaniko who told me that the owner of the building has closed the hotel in a dispute with residents who did not agree with his vision for the future of Shaniko. The town will continue to fade away, as it is at this writing, unless the hotel reopens. One can only hope for a positive resolution so that Shaniko can reclaim its place as one of the best ghost towns of Oregon.

Across the street from that now-shuttered hotel to the south are several clapboard false-front structures, including the former Gold Nugget Saloon, built in 1901.

At the rear of the 1901 city hall, which stands east of the hotel, is the town's three-cell jail, a wooden structure with boards laid flat, stockade-style, for stoutness. The cells were given names by early occupants: "The Snake Pit," "The Bum-lodging," and "The Palace-sleeper." The building also served as the town's firehouse.

The largest structure in Shaniko is the tin-covered wool shed, which stands east of town. The railroad tracks ran immediately east of the structure, and the depot stood north of the shed.

Shaniko's three-room clapboard school, built in 1901, features an unusual octagonal bell tower.

The 1901 water tower, northwest of the business district, is Shaniko's most imposing structure. Water was pumped from a spring south of Shaniko to two ten-thousand-gallon wooden tanks located seventy feet up inside the tower.

East of the water tower is the three-room, clapboard 1901 school, which has an unusual octagonal bell tower. I have seen it painted white and saw a picture of it when it was yellow, but it is now a light green, which was the authentic original color. This was determined when unfaded boards were discovered below the school's floor level.

Shaniko, surprisingly, has no cemetery. The ground was too hard for one.

About a half-mile south of Shaniko on the road to Antelope, a double-cupola barn on the west side of the road stands as the last remnant of the area's original town, Cross Hollows.

WHEN YOU GO

Shaniko is 15.5 miles south of Kent on U.S. Highway 97.

ANTELOPE

Antelope Valley was named in 1862 by freighters of a supply train who saw herds of antelope while carrying goods to the recently discovered gold fields at what would become Sumpter, Granite, and Bourne, all now ghost towns in northeastern Oregon and featured in the next chapter. The town that developed in Antelope Valley took Antelope as its name when a post office was granted in 1871. It became a commercial center for ranchers and sheepherders until the Columbia Southern Railroad extended tracks south from Biggs Junction and Shaniko came into being. The new town took most of the commerce from Antelope.

When I first visited Antelope in 1982, it was a place of both peace and turmoil. The peace came from the apparent—and the key word is apparent—bliss experienced by the majority of the town's population, who were followers of Bhagwan Shree Rajneesh. The turmoil came from the resentment felt by residents who had lived there before the arrival of the Bhagwan and his devotees in 1981. They watched Antelope being taken over and radically changed. The town's name became Rajneesh, and the

The vacant Antelope Garage features ornamental tin on its front and sides.

Antelope's Ancient Order of United Workmen Hall, built in 1898, appears at this writing to be a private residence.

only restaurant/store became Zorba the Buddha Restaurant. The town was featured on national news programs as the silent Bhagwan's spokesperson, Ma Anand Sheela, defended the cult's policies. She eventually fled the country, allegedly with considerable amounts of money, and the Bhagwan himself was deported in 1985 on charges of immigration fraud. With the departure of the Bhagwan and his followers, the town unanimously voted to return the town's name to Antelope and then promptly disincorporated to avoid a recurrence.

WALKING AND DRIVING AROUND ANTELOPE

Antelope today has returned to its pre-Bhagwan existence. It consists of several very photogenic buildings, the most striking of which is the 1897 Methodist church at Union and College Streets, one block east of downtown's Main Street. On Main Street, south of Union, stands the tiny former office of Antelope's newspaper, the *Herald*. Across the street from the newspaper is an old Shell station with its signature white, yellow, and red banding below its windows. If you look carefully, you can still read "SHELL" on its fading false front. South of the Shell station stands the two-story Ancient Order of United Workmen (AOUW) Hall, built in 1898. South of the AOUW hall is the former Antelope Garage, which

Antelope's 1897 Methodist church looks strikingly similar to the abandoned church in Grass Valley (see page 134).

features a tin false front with several hard-to-read signs, one bleeding into the other, except for one that establishes clearly that it was a Union 76 station.

Antelope's largest but least attractive building, located on the north end of town off McGreer Street, is its former public school. When it was being erected, I'll bet some of the parishioners at the graceful, lovely church down the street cringed as they saw what the school would become. If I could categorize its style, I think it might be institutional mundane.

The Antelope Cemetery is quite large but rather sparsely populated, as if townspeople expected Antelope to be much bigger than it turned out to be.

The compound that Bahgwan Shree Rajneesh built for his followers is now the Washington Family Ranch, a Young Life Christian camp. As one local resident told me, "That place has gone from very bad to very good—but then so has the town."

WHEN YOU GO

Antelope is 7.9 miles south of Shaniko on Oregon Highway 218, the Shaniko–Fossil Highway. The cemetery is 0.4 of a mile east of town, off of Union Street.

MAYVILLE

Originally known as Clyde for a local blacksmith, Mayville was settled in the late 1870s. It took its present name at about the time it was granted a post office in 1884. The community eventually featured a hotel, a general store, a grist mill, an Odd Fellows hall, and a two-room school, located about a mile north of town. When the need for a high school classroom arose, a third room was added to the school.

WALKING AND DRIVING AROUND MAYVILLE

The premier building in Mayville today is the 1895 IOOF Hall, the second in Mayville's history, having replaced an earlier one that burned. The building still has its outdoor stairway to the second floor, unlike the hall in Kent. Two other false-front buildings stand in town along with a residence that appears to have been converted from a service station. Farther north is a sagging, one-story commercial building, and on the south end of town is a two-story, boarded-up residence with a pyramidal roof.

The Mayville Cemetery, originally the IOOF Cemetery, was established in 1886. It has a magnificent view of Mount Hood. The headstone for Henry Beck (1842–1899) has the most dismal epitaph I have ever read in my almost forty years of ghost town hunting:

Poorly born, Poorly lived
Poorly died, and no one cried.

WHEN YOU GO

Mayville is 41.4 miles northeast of Antelope. From Antelope, take Oregon Highway 218 for 34.3 miles east to Fossil. (Be sure to see the 1901 Wheeler County Courthouse on Adams Street in Fossil.) Turn left in Fossil onto Oregon Highway 19. Mayville is 7.1 miles north of Fossil on Highway 19.

To reach the Mayville Cemetery, go north of town 0.8 of a mile and head west on Cemetery Road for 0.5 of a mile.

The largest building in Mayville is the 1895 Odd Fellows Hall, which features an external stairway to the IOOF meeting hall on the second floor. Usually the first floor of such lodges served an unrelated commercial purpose.

Across the street from Mayville's Odd Fellows Hall stands what appears to have been a vehicle repair garage.

The grave of Henry Beck, in the Mayville Cemetery, contains the most forlorn epitaph I have ever read: *Poorly Born / Poorly Lived / Poorly Died, / and no one cried.*

LONEROCK

When Lone Rock Valley was settled beginning in 1871, the town of Lone Rock became the first incorporated town in Gilliam County. When the postal service granted a post office in 1875, the name was shortened to one word.

WALKING AND DRIVING AROUND LONEROCK

The business district of this still-living, but isolated, town features several older wooden buildings. One structure that now serves as the community hall has a clapboard false front, but board-and-batten sides.

On the southwest side of town is the old jail, built in 1891 of boards laid flat. The door is also wooden, but it has huge hinges and an impressive hasp.

The large, two-story residence on the east end of town is the former schoolhouse, now missing its large center belfry, which was built in 1903 and accommodated all twelve grades. The last high school class graduated in 1932, and the school closed for good in 1961.

To learn why the town received its name, visit the attractive Methodist church and its parsonage, both dating from 1898. Behind the church is an enormous, solitary boulder.

The Lonerock Cemetery is not visible from town, but it has a fine view of the surrounding valley and so is worth seeking out.

Lonerock's 1891 wooden jail, with boards laid flat for stoutness, hasn't been entered in quite a while. Note the dense web across the latch.

Looming behind the 1898 Methodist church in Lonerock is the huge boulder for which the town is named.

The Lonerock Community Hall is a classic example of a commercial building with a clapboard false front.

WHEN YOU GO

Lonerock is 33.1 miles east of Mayville. From Mayville, drive north on Oregon Highway 19 for 12 miles to Condon. Turn east on Oregon Highway 206 and proceed for 4.7 miles. From there, take Lonerock Road 16.4 miles southeast to the town. The road becomes a very good dirt road for 3.7 miles before entering Lonerock.

To reach the cemetery, follow Lonerock Road south from the church for 1.8 miles, turn left on Campbell Lane, and proceed 1.2 miles to the cemetery, on a hill to your left.

HARDMAN

Hardman is one of Oregon's most picturesque towns, a prairie ghost of several dozen wonderful, weathered, wooden buildings—fewer than half of them in use—surrounded by wheat fields and grasslands.

Dairyville was a small stop along a popular stage and freight route in the 1860s. Popularly known as Raw Dog, the town even had a small rival up the road, known as Yallerdog. The two towns eventually combined into one, informally called Dog Town. A nearby farmer named David Hardman had been operating a small post office from his home, and when he moved into town, he brought the post office with him. Dairyville–Raw Dog–Dog Town became Hardman.

Hardman developed as a milling center for area wheat farmers, and the popular freight route brought hotels and modest prosperity in the early 1900s. But the same railroads that made Dufur, Friend, Kent, and Shaniko prominent ignored Hardman, and the town went into a gradual decline.

Across the street from the community center in Hardman stands a former grocery store and gas station.

The Hardman Community Center was originally the IOOF Hall, built in 1870. Notice the elaborately jigged ornamental brackets that decorate the building's cornice.

WALKING AND DRIVING AROUND HARDMAN

On one of my several visits to Hardman, I met a young man who was dedicated to the preservation of this photogenic town. I said at the time that what the town really needed was assistance from the state or a national historic grant to preserve the site. He told me that what the town *really* needed was a fire truck. The nearest is in Heppner, some twenty miles away. I looked around at the surrounding dry fields and couldn't have agreed more.

The keystone building in Hardman today is the 1870 community center, formerly the IOOF Hall. On my third of four visits to Hardman, in 2003, I was fortunate enough to find the normally locked building open for a rummage sale. The structure features a stage at the back and an attached kitchen. The building is used for wedding receptions and other social occasions. Several photographs hang on the walls, including one of an overview of Hardman taken in about 1900.

Smaller structures stretch north from the hall, the first of which was the former post office. Attached to it is a deserted residence with a string of rural postal boxes extending north along the highway. A one-time gas station and grocery store stands across the street. Residences are scattered on back streets on both sides of the highway.

Immediately north of Hardman's community center is the former post office, along with the mailboxes of the town's few residents.

The cemetery is on a hill 0.2 of a mile southwest of the community center. In it stand five headstones in a large, fenced-off area. One of the graves is for Sina Emry, who died on November 19, 1892, in her forty-first year. Buried next to Emry—with a headstone so close that at first it appears attached to hers—is her infant son, who died the day before she did. In 1892, being pregnant at age forty was perilous, indeed.

A second cemetery, the IOOF, is 4.1 miles northwest of town on Hardman Ridge Road. The graveyard is off to the left of the road.

WHEN YOU GO

*Hardman is 22.5 miles northeast of Lonerock, all but the last 0.2 of a mile on good dirt roads. From Lonerock, drive 12.9 miles north on the very scenic Buttermilk Canyon Road to Hale Ridge Road. Turn right and head east for 3 miles, where Hardman Ridge Road goes straight and then heads southeast for 6.1 miles to Oregon Highway 207, also known as the Heppner–Spray Highway. Turn right onto the paved highway and proceed 0.2 miles into Hardman. (**Note:** The nearest place for gas or supplies is Heppner, a pleasant community 19.6 miles northeast of Hardman.)*

RICHMOND

Richmond is well off the logical route as you travel to the ghost towns in this chapter, and it only features two buildings you can actually visit. However, like Sherman and Govan in chapter 2, I still consider the site worth taking a side trip to see it.

Ranchers and farmers founded Richmond in 1890 because no permanent community existed near their holdings. The first structure built was a school, followed by a store and a church. Named for the capital of the Confederacy, Richmond enjoyed a modest prosperity until the advent of the automobile, when a day's buggy ride became a short jaunt in a car. Distant towns were no longer distant, and Richmond withered.

The school, store, and church built in 1890 still stand. As you enter the tiny community from the highway, the long, deteriorating, wooden building on your

left served as a combination store, post office, and residence. Only partially visible across the street is the former Methodist church, which still sports its bell in the belfry. It stands on private property.

No doubt once an elegant residence in Richmond, this two-story home featured large, now-collapsed, roofed porches. Note that there was a later attempt to preserve the building with a metal roof, an effort that has obviously failed.

South of the church, even more hidden by brush, is the school, also on private property, which closed in 1952. The school at one time had a stable to accommodate students who needed to ride to classes. In its heyday, the one-room school had one teacher and forty students, grades one through eight. In its last year of service, the school still had one teacher, but there was also only one student. The last time I viewed the school, in 2003, the school had lost its bell but still had its blackboards. When I visited Richmond in 2011, I was denied access to the church and the school.

If you wish to see the pews from the church and the desks from the school, I was told that you will find them in a museum in Fossil.

The well-preserved 1874 Waldron School stands 3.6 miles south of the turnoff to Richmond on Oregon Highway 27.

I was denied permission to photograph the former Richmond School in 2011. I took this photo in 2003, when local resident Rob Donnelly gave me a thorough tour of the community. The school looks little different now than it did that year.

The Methodist church in Richmond is now a private residence. As with the school, I was denied permission to photograph it in 2011. It looks much the same as it did when I took this photo in 2003.

Richmond is 54.3 miles southwest of Hardman. From Hardman, drive 47.4 miles south and then west on Oregon Highway 207, going through the small community of Spray on the way. Turn left (south) at the point that Oregon Highway 19 heads northwest and Oregon Highway 207 turns south (now also marked as the Service Creek–Mitchell Highway), and go 5.5 miles to the clearly marked turnoff to Richmond on Richmond–Sixshooter Road. The town is 0.9 of a mile east of that turnoff.

6

GHOSTS

O F

NORTH-EASTERN OREGON

THE OREGON BACKROADS ADVENTURE begun in chapter 5 continues in this chapter. Once again, you will explore some true ghost towns and historic spots that most out-of-state tourists—as well as many Oregon natives—have overlooked.

All the towns in this chapter except the final one were greatly affected by the Sumpter Valley Railway, affectionately known as the Stump Dodger, which extended from Baker City toward the gold mines of Sumpter. Begun in 1890, it was completed the following year to McEwen, five miles southeast of Sumpter. It reached Sumpter in 1896. A second, much longer line proceeded west from McEwen toward Whitney in 1899 and eventually extended all the way to Prairie City, about eighty miles from Baker City. For all these towns and for others along the route, the railroad was the lifeline, carrying logs, lumber, freight, livestock, gold, and passengers. By the time the railroad was abandoned in 1947, the communities of the region were in serious decline.

The Flora Cemetery, in Flora, Oregon, features a beautiful metal arch over its gate.

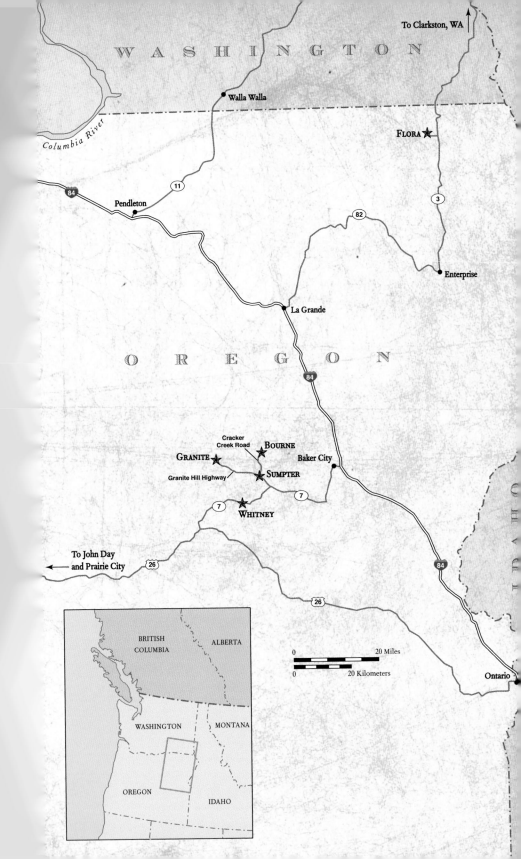

WHITNEY

Whitney came into being in 1901 when the Sumpter Valley Railway reached the Whitney Valley, named for pioneer C. H. Whitney. Logging railroads eventually expanded in all directions from the community, which also served as the center for stage lines that connected mining and ranching towns in the vicinity. Whitney was a lumber company town, but many of its residents were connected with the railroad, which had a roundhouse there. The community's prosperity came to an end with the railroad's abandonment in 1947.

WALKING AND DRIVING AROUND WHITNEY

About twenty buildings still stand in Whitney today, all very simple in design and construction. Only two of the town's residences appear to be occupied at this writing.

A 1938 sawmill built by the Nibley Lumber Company was still standing in its spectral beauty south of town when the first edition of this book debuted in 2005. Unfortunately, it has collapsed, and its ruins have been removed.

The lumber town of Whitney has several cabins and outbuildings made both of logs and milled wood.

The Whitney Cemetery sits in isolation off Oregon Highway 7. Several fences surround unmarked graves, but only two headstones remain.

The tiny Whitney Cemetery northeast of town is set off by a buck-rail fence. Six individual picket fences mark gravesites, but only two markers, both for children, remain.

WHEN YOU GO

Whitney is 132 miles east of Richmond, the final entry of chapter 5. From Richmond, return 0.9 of a mile to Oregon Highway 207 and head south for 18.3 miles to the community of Mitchell, which is at the junction of Highway 207 and U.S. Highway 26. Drive east on U.S. 26 for 69.2 miles to the town of John Day.

From John Day, drive 28.3 miles east on U.S. 26 to the junction with Oregon Highway 7. Take that highway northeast to Whitney, a distance of 15.2 miles.

To see the Whitney Cemetery, take Oregon Highway 7 northeast from Whitney for 0.7 of a mile and turn left onto Forest Service Road 1055. In 0.1 of a mile, take a track to the left; the cemetery's fence will already be visible.

SUMPTER

In 1862, five southerners found gold in Oregon's Blue Mountains. They named the town that grew near their claims Fort Sumter, after the site of the first Confederate victory in the Civil War. Early placer deposits were modest, and success was sporadic until the 1880s, when hard rock mining began. When a post office was granted in 1883, officials in Washington likely surmised the Confederate origins of the name, because "Fort" was dropped and the spelling was altered to "Sumpter."

The Sumpter Valley Railway reached the town from Baker City in 1896. Sumpter's population peaked at about 3,500, and by 1899 it featured eleven hotels, eleven general mercantiles, and seventeen saloons, along with various other enterprises.

By 1906, mines began to close, and prices of real estate in town plummeted. A smelter that was erected in 1903 shut down in 1908. The town seemed doomed, but only five years later, the seemingly moribund town found new life when dredging operations began and, except for being shut down during World War II, lasted until 1954, greatly prolonging the life of Sumpter.

Heisler locomotive No. 3 sits at the depot in Sumpter. Built in 1915, the engine served the W. H. Eccles Lumber Company on branch lines off the Sumpter Valley main line.

WALKING AND DRIVING AROUND SUMPTER

Sumpter is currently home to almost two hundred people. Mill Street, the main street through town, contains several historic buildings and many modern ones. Actually, "historic" is relative; few buildings date to the town's origins, since eleven city blocks, including nine brick buildings, burned in 1917.

The Sumpter Municipal Museum is one of the more photogenic structures on Mill Street. Formerly Sumpter Supply, it is housed in two side-by-side brick buildings.

Near the north end of town stands the two-story, brick Sumpter Trading Post, which originally was Basche's Hardware. Built in 1899, it burned in the fire of 1917 but was rebuilt four years later.

Another historic building, one block east of Main on Columbia Street, was built in 1900 as the Sumpter General Hospital; it is now a bed and breakfast establishment. The two-story clapboard structure survived the great fire only because the conflagration was contained across the street. Masons purchased the building in 1918 because their lodge had perished in the fire. They used the former hospital as a lodge for fifty-five years.

Sumpter features two enjoyable tourist attractions. One is the Sumpter Valley Railway, a steam-powered narrow gauge line that runs between

A 1913 fire destroyed the building that once surrounded this vault. A much larger fire destroyed most of downtown Sumpter in 1917. Notice the cache of "gold" stashed inside.

Sumpter Dredge No. 3, abandoned in a pond of its own making in 1954, has become a major tourist attraction in the Sumpter Valley.

Sumpter and McEwen on weekends and holidays from Memorial Day through September. The line's 1915 Heisler locomotive is one of very few operating wood-burning engines in regular service in the United States today.

The other attraction stands at the south end of town: Sumpter Dredge No. 3, a 1,250-ton behemoth that remains where it was abandoned in 1954. It was launched in 1935, built primarily from parts salvaged from earlier dredges that had been idle for a decade. These dredges traveled more than eight miles in their mining efforts and reclaimed between $10 million and $12 million in gold from the riverbeds. Dredge No. 3 is more complete than most, because abandoned dredges were salvaged for scrap, many during World War II. This one is not, however, entirely complete: For example, the electric motor that powered the digging winch is missing. Despite its idleness, the dredge still smells of grease and fuel. (There is no charge to tour the dredge, although donations are accepted.)

Since dredges are so rare, here is a primer on the subject: A dredge is a digging apparatus located on a flat-bottomed boat. It is constructed on land and then

The Sumpter Municipal Museum and public library is housed in the former Sumpter Supply building.

183

John Beardsley's tree stump headstone in Sumpter's Blue Mountain Cemetery establishes that he was a member of the Woodmen of the World, a fraternal organization.

Sumpter General Hospital, built in 1900, now operates as a bed and breakfast inn.

launched into a pond created for it. It then digs its way along, floating on the extended pond it creates with its massive buckets. Dredge No. 3's buckets, seventy-two in number, each weigh one ton. They are connected to a huge "digging ladder" that scoops into the pond. Through an elaborate screening process, gold-bearing sand or gravel is separated from rock, and the detritus is sent out the rear of the dredge, creating enormous piles behind the contraption.

Though not exactly a tourist attraction, Sumpter also has an interesting graveyard, the Blue Mountain Cemetery. Those of us who wander through old cemeteries are accustomed to reading stones that pose more questions than they answer. I found one headstone near the northern boundary of the Blue Mountain Cemetery most disturbing. It has the names of three people: Clara E. (born in Posen, Germany), Willy Gustav, and Ella M., wife and children, respectively, of Ernst Maiwaldt. Clara, his wife, was thirty-four. Willy never saw his third birthday. Ella lived for little more than two months. They all died on the same day: April 26, 1895. Illness? Fire? Buggy accident? One tries to imagine the husband and father's grief.

WHEN YOU GO

Sumpter is northeast of Whitney. From Whitney, drive 9.7 miles northeast on Oregon Highway 7. Turn left on Oregon Highway 410 (the Sumpter Valley Highway) and drive 3.1 miles into Sumpter.

If you wish to visit Sumpter's Blue Mountain Cemetery, take Mill Street to Austin Street. Head southeast for 1.4 miles on Austin, which becomes Sumpter Cemetery Road.

GRANITE

Granite came into being when a party led by Albert Gallatin Tabor and scout Robert W. Waucop found gold in a gulch on July 4, 1862. Tabor appropriately named his claim the Independence, and the town that grew at the site took the same name. When a post office was granted in 1876, an Independence, Oregon, already existed near Salem, so the town's name was changed to Granite. A. G. Tabor served as the first postmaster.

By 1900, Granite consisted of a drugstore, three other stores, five saloons, and two hotels, including the three-story Grand Hotel, which had dining facilities, a bar, and forty-two rooms. Many Civil War veterans and citizens originally from Italy, France, the Netherlands, Sweden, and Ireland populated the town. Ladies in town formed the Daughters of Progress, which created a library and helped form religious societies.

The Cougar–Independence and Buffalo mines were solid gold producers for decades. The town at first flourished—but eventually only subsisted—as the supply center for area mines into the 1950s. The Grand Hotel served meals into the late 1930s but was demolished in about 1943 as Granite slid into decline. The post office closed in 1957.

WALKING AND DRIVING AROUND GRANITE

When you enter Granite today, you drive up Center Street past Allen Hall, a board-and-batten combination city hall and one-room school. The bell tower of the building is unusual because it is only framework rather than an enclosed structure. A larger school closed for lack of students in the 1940s and burned in the 1950s.

On the northwest corner of Center and Main Streets stands the J. J. O'Dair Store, a large general merchandise with a white, clapboard false front and a front door on the diagonal. An advertisement in the local newspaper, the *Granite Gem*, touted the store in 1900: "Sells the cheapest. Carries a full line of groceries and dry goods. New goods constantly arriving and we are prepared to fill any and all orders."

South of the O'Dair Store on the opposite side of Main Street is the boarded-up dance hall and saloon, featuring an unusual shingle pattern under the cornice and decorative trim on the second-floor windows. The elegant Grand Hotel formerly stood across the street.

Granite's Allen Hall has an unusual belfry in that it is only framework rather than being enclosed.

The J. J. O'Dair Store in Granite would be a fairly standard clapboard, false-front building were it not for its front door set jauntily on the diagonal.

Across the street east of the O'Dair Store stands the 1901 drugstore, now a residence. The former Catholic church, across from the drugstore, is also a residence. Down the hill behind the former church is the attractive cemetery, which features dozens of well-carved headstones of antiquity, including one for gold discoverer A. G. Tabor. As mentioned before, he made his gold discovery on Independence Day. Coincidentally, he also died on that day—in 1892.

WHEN YOU GO

Granite is 16.5 miles northwest of Sumpter on Oregon Highway 220, the Granite Hill Highway, which is the main street heading out of Sumpter.

A cabin in Granite features logs with chinking for the main part of the structure, but a board-and-batten addition makes up the rear of the building.

BOURNE

Bourne didn't shine as brightly as either Sumpter or Granite, and today it is a minor site with a few old buildings—some vacant, some in heaps—and a few newer, occupied cabins.

When gold was found along Cracker Creek north of the excitement at Sumpter, the community of 1,500 people that formed there was originally named Cracker. When a post office was granted in 1895, the town's name was changed to honor Jonathan Bourne of

The sparse ruins of a dredge sit in its own bog along Cracker Creek Road on the way to Bourne. Its waste gravel piles stand behind the wreckage.

Portland, who owned the nearby Eureka and Excelsior Mine. He later served Oregon for one term in the U.S. Senate.

James Waucop "Walkie" Tabor, whose father was the founder of Granite, owned a general merchandise in Bourne in the early 1920s, and his wife Margaret was the postmistress. By that time Bourne's population was less than a hundred. Bourne lost its post office in 1927 and nearly lost everything else in 1937 when a flood took out most of the town.

The very passable dirt road up to Bourne features constant evidence of the dredging of Cracker Creek, and the scant remnants of an old dredge, sitting in its bog, stands 1.2 miles north of the junction of Cracker Creek Road and the Granite Hill Highway on the right side of the road. When you look at this wreck, which is more representative

A small, metal sign above the door of this vacant residence in Bourne identifies the one-time occupant as Edward Konka. Four holes, which appear to be cotes for birds, have been cut into the gable near the apex of the roof.

of the current state of dredges in the West, you might further appreciate the remarkable condition of Sumpter Dredge No. 3.

Bourne is 6.2 miles north of Sumpter on Cracker Creek Road, which leaves Granite Hill Road just west of Sumpter. At 4.8 miles, there is an unmarked split in the road; take the right fork to Bourne.

FLORA

Once a town of 1,200, Flora currently has a population of seven. Although it's located far from the other sites in this chapter, I highly recommend a visit, as Flora is one of Oregon's most delightful ghost towns, containing some extremely photogenic buildings.

Originally called Johnson Meadow for pioneer homesteader Frank Johnson, the community became Flora when a post office was granted in 1890. It was named for then-six-year-old Flora Buzzard, daughter of the first postmaster, Adolphus Buzzard.

The agricultural community soon featured a school, a general store, a lumber company, a blacksmith's shop, a hotel, two churches—and no saloons.

The town prospered until after World War I, when its isolation from major markets and the decline of the small family farm caused a population decrease. The post office closed in 1966; the school shut its doors in 1977.

The Flora School, built in 1915, now serves as the Flora Education Center, primarily for adults.

Flora's 1898 Methodist Episcopal church stands in the foreground with the 1915 Flora School behind it.

A two-story residence in Flora embodies what people want to see when they visit a ghost town.

WALKING AND DRIVING AROUND FLORA

The two most striking structures in town today are the 1898 Methodist Episcopal church and the Flora School, which stand near each other on the north side of town. The two-story clapboard school, erected in 1915, has a shingled bell tower topped with a flagpole. It has been restored since I first saw it in 2000 and now serves as the Flora School Education Center, which has programs in folk arts and historic agriculture, centering on skills that were crucial to the original homesteaders in the area.

One rather curious thing about the Flora Cemetery, west of the main part of town, is that most of its headstones face west, with graves east of them. Therefore, instead of standing at the foot of a grave to read the stone's inscription, you must stand behind the head of the grave to read it.

WHEN YOU GO

Flora is 172 miles northeast of Sumpter. From Sumpter, head south on Oregon Highway 220 to Oregon Highway 7 and turn left (east). Drive 27.2 miles through Baker City to Interstate 84. Take Interstate 84 for 41.9 miles north to La Grande. From La Grande, take Oregon Highway 82 northeast to Enterprise, a distance of 63.3 miles. In Enterprise, go north on Oregon Highway 3 for 33.6 miles, where the turnoff to Flora is clearly marked. Flora is 2.7 miles west of Oregon Highway 3.

The Flora Cemetery is 0.3 of a mile northwest of the school, where Flora Lane, the main road through town, makes a ninety-degree turn to the west and becomes Lost Prairie Road.

7 GHOSTS OF SOUTH-WESTERN OREGON

TWO DESERTED GHOST TOWNS, a vanished site with a touching cemetery, a minor semighost, and an historic gem of a community lie near Grants Pass and Medford. Although they are geographically far removed from the rest of the sites in this book, Buncom, Golden, Sterlingville, Kerby, and remarkable Jacksonville are well worth traveling the distance.

The weather-worn church door in Golden shows its age, as does this elegant handle and facing plate.

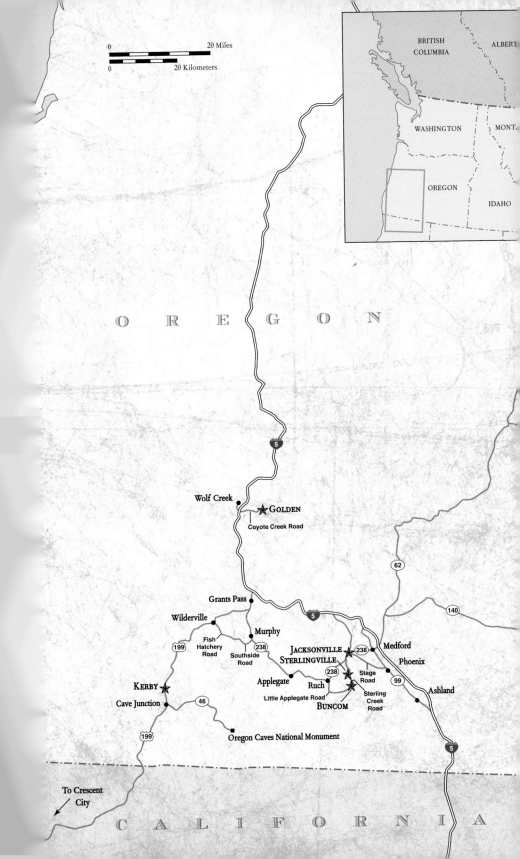

JACKSONVILLE

Gold was first found in southern Oregon in 1851, but the word didn't really get out until the spring of 1852 when James Gluggage and James Pool found gold at a place that they would appropriately call Rich Gulch. Within a matter of months, the rush was on to a new boomtown called Table Rock City, named for a nearby mesa.

The community was the only town within Jackson County, which had been formed in January of that same year. Table Rock City, renamed Jacksonville, became the county seat in 1853. Both county and town were apparently named for former President Andrew Jackson, who symbolized for Oregonians the virtues of the American frontier.

Jacksonville may have had the virtues of the frontier, but it also had the vices. One Methodist minister lamented that he received complaints from a nearby saloon that his parishioners' singing and praying were annoying the saloon's customers.

Gold mining declined in the 1860s, but the town nevertheless prospered as a trading center. When fires swept through downtown in 1873 and 1874, the city passed an ordinance that downtown buildings be constructed of brick.

Jacksonville's Redmen's Hall, with its fading advertisements, heads a string of excellent brick buildings on California Street.

The Jeremiah Nunan House, built in 1893, is the showplace residence in Jacksonville. At this writing, it serves as a bed and breakfast inn.

In 1886, the Oregon & California Railroad bypassed the town, and Medford was born. Jacksonville attempted to soften the blow in 1891 by constructing the Rogue River Valley Railway to Medford, but by that time Medford was already outpacing Jacksonville. The former pride of Jackson County was slipping into decline. The final blow came in 1927 when upstart Medford took the Jackson County seat.

WALKING AND DRIVING AROUND JACKSONVILLE

Jacksonville was designated a National Historic Landmark in 1967. Almost everything within the enchanting town is easily reached on foot, and a handy walking tour map is available at the Visitor Information Center at Oregon and C Streets.

The core of the action in Jacksonville is on California Street, Oregon Highway 238 through town, or on side streets near California. The historic buildings are too numerous to include here, but these are a few favorites of mine. On the south side of California Street are twin two-story buildings with beautifully crafted brick patterns, the Redmen's Hall and the K. Kubli Building, both built in 1884. The east wall of the Redmen's Hall also features fading advertisements that are challenging to read, as some partially bleed over others.

On the north side of California Street, one block east of the Redmen's Hall, stand the 1863 Beekman Bank, the first bank in southern Oregon, and the 1880 United States Hotel. President Rutherford B. Hayes and his party, including General William Tecumseh Sherman, spent the night there before it was quite completed. As a Republican, President Hayes apparently received a cool reception in the largely Democratic town. Local lore has it that after being charged more than double the going rate of San Francisco's finest hotels, General Sherman remarked that they merely wished to spend the night, not purchase the establishment.

A one-story former butcher shop, built in 1854 by John Orth, stands on the southwest corner of California and Oregon Streets. Orth clearly was successful in his endeavors, as next door he built the 1872 J. Orth Building, a handsome two-story brick edifice with a second-story balcony over its first-floor porch.

If you walk south on Oregon beyond the Orth Building, you'll come upon the 1880-81 City Hall, which is still set up for town meetings. The building also housed the office of the town recorder, two jail cells, and, in the rear, a firehouse. One block east of the city hall is further testament to Orth's success—the 1880 Orth House, now a bed and breakfast inn.

The 1883 Jackson County Courthouse, located east of downtown on Fifth Street, now houses the Jacksonville Museum. The former courthouse, once called "The Crown Jewel of Jackson County," offers displays on the mining, logging, and sheepherding industries.

Next door to the courthouse stands the 1911 county jail, which has served as a children's museum since 1979. Inside I found young people busily learning about domestic pioneer life on the first floor, while on the second floor children were exploring hands-on exhibits depicting such businesses as a bank, a barber shop, a garage, and a milliner's shop.

Of all the attractive churches in Jacksonville, my favorite is on the corner of California and Sixth Streets, one block southeast of the courthouse. The graceful 1881 First Presbyterian Church, constructed of sugar pine from Roseburg, a hundred miles north of Jacksonville, features elaborate trim and a steep, slim steeple. Even the chimney is ornately decorated.

One block east of that church on the south side of California Street is one of the premier residences in town, the Gothic-style Beekman House, built around 1870. Cornelius C. Beekman was the owner of the Beekman Bank and

Jacksonville's First Presbyterian Church was constructed in 1881 with sugar pine from Roseburg, almost one hundred miles away.

one of the town's prominent citizens. The house has living-history inhabitants in 1911 period dress to help you time travel to an earlier Jacksonville.

You might want your car for the final two stops. The first is the Jacksonville Cemetery, located at the end of Cemetery Lane, three blocks north of California on Oregon Street. The lane climbs above the town into a huge and fascinating graveyard that actually consists of six distinct and separate cemeteries: The City, Jewish, and Catholic sections, and sections for three fraternal organizations—the Odd Fellows, Masons, and Redmen. The cemetery is one of the best in the American West because of its tree-filled beauty and its many older stones. A person could spend hours wandering through the Jacksonville Cemetery, but an automobile is the easiest way to navigate it.

Just on your left as you drive up to the beginning of the cemetery is the area for banker Cornelius C. Beekman and his family. Nearby are members of the Nunan family, whose house you will visit next.

Willie and Leah Robinson, ages six and five years, respectively, and buried in the Jacksonville Cemetery, died five days apart in 1890. Their epitaph, with a small subject-verb agreement problem, reads: *Here rests the sweetest buds of hope/That ere to human hearts were given.*

German native John Neuber, who died in Jacksonville in 1875 at forty-six years of age, has the simplest epitaph of all: *Hope.*

The Jacksonville Cemetery contains hundreds of headstones of antiquity, including elaborate monuments for the town's wealthiest citizens.

One touching marker among hundreds of headstones is for Myra E. Simpkins, who was born in 1865, married in 1891, and died in 1892:

> *Ah! Life is brief, though love is long,*
> *The altar and the bier;*
> *The burial hymn and bridal song*
> *Were all in one short year.*

To reach the next attraction, return from the cemetery to Oregon Street and turn north. In 0.2 of a mile you will see the Nunan House on your left. Erected in 1893, the elaborate residence, now a bed and breakfast inn, was ordered by prominent merchant Jeremiah Nunan from a plan book of a Tennessee architect, and building materials arrived by train from the eastern United States.

WHEN YOU GO

Jacksonville is 562 miles southwest of Flora, the last ghost town in chapter 6. Most routes between the two towns bring you near to marvelous Crater Lake, Oregon's only National Park.

Jacksonville is 5 miles southwest of Medford on Oregon Highway 238.

THE STERLINGVILLE CEMETERY

The 1860s placer mining community of Sterlingville, once the site of the largest hydraulic mine in the state, has completely disappeared except for its cemetery. In the northeast corner of that graveyard is one of the most stirring headstones I have ever seen. It is a marker for Mary E. Saltmarsh, who died in 1878 at forty-three years of age. The marker also lists her ten children, none of whom passed the age of ten. Many were stillborn, or lived a day, or died in infancy. Basically, a child of hers died almost every two years, and her last child died in the same year she did. I cannot remember a stone relating such continuing sorrow. Her husband, incidentally, outlived her by twenty-eight years and died at eighty-one years of age.

West of Mary Saltmarsh's grave is a small mystery. Three stones for siblings Albert, Lettie, and Aaron Yaudes stand together. The

children were born in 1873, 1875, and 1879, respectively. They all died on the same day: May 23, 1884. One can only speculate on the cause—and know that on that day there was great mourning in Sterlingville.

The Sterlingville Cemetery is 8.3 miles south of Jacksonville. In Jacksonville, turn south from California Street (Oregon Highway 238) onto Oregon Street. In 0.2 of a mile, turn left on Applegate Street. Applegate heads out of town and becomes Cady Road. Follow Cady Road southwest for 1.8 miles. Turn left (southeast) onto Sterling Creek Road, which leads you in 6.3 miles to the marked turnoff to the Sterlingville Cemetery.

The Sterlingville Cemetery grave of Mary Saltmarsh, in addition to her name, lists her ten children, who all preceded her in death.

BUNCOM

Buncom is a tiny, deserted site south of Jacksonville. The two towns clearly demonstrate the extremes of the sites in the Pacific Northwest: Jacksonville is an historic, charming place but has few true ghost town elements. Buncom, on the other hand, is the essence of what the true ghost town fan seeks: old buildings in peaceful isolation.

Buncom was originally a gold camp settled in the 1850s and 1860s. The origin of the town's name is not known for certain, but it is likely that early miners found little of promise and so dubbed the place a "bunkum," miner's slang for "something of little worth." The community's name was variously spelled Bunkum, Buncom, Bunkomville, and, perhaps to add gentility with a glossier spelling, Buncombe.

After a modest amount of placer gold played out, Buncom hung on as a farming, ranching, and logging center into the 1930s.

WALKING AROUND BUNCOM

In Buncom today stand three aging buildings under roof. A small board-and-batten building dating from about 1896 served as the post office. Next door to the post office is the bunkhouse of the Federal Mining Company, and across the street stands the company's cookhouse, later used as a barn. Both the bunkhouse and the one-time cookhouse probably date from the 1920s.

A local resident told me that Buncom shines once a year, on Memorial Day weekend, for Buncom Days. He said they have a parade, but it's so short that they run it up and back a few times so everyone gets to enjoy it.

All three of Buncom's buildings are seen in this photograph. In the foreground is a cookhouse, later used as a barn. In the right rear stands the board-and-batten post office and to the left is the bunkhouse of the Federal Mining Company, also of board-and-batten construction.

WHEN YOU GO

Buncom is 4.3 miles beyond the Sterlingville Cemetery on Sterling Creek Road.

KERBY

In 1856, Josephine County was created from the western section of Jackson County, and the county seat was established at Waldo (now a virtually vanished mining community on private property). The county was named for Josephine Rollins, daughter of a local miner. In December of that same year, Canada native Dr. D. S. Holton purchased a land claim from James Kerby and built a house on the property. That house became the first building in Kerbyville. A year later, Kerbyville took the county seat from Waldo.

The principal attraction in Kerby is its museum. The Stith-Naucke residence, built in 1871, is open for inspection at the museum and is filled with period furniture, implements, and clothing.

The pantry of the Stith-Naucke home displays everyday kitchen items from the nineteenth century.

With rich placer gold deposits along the nearby Illinois River, Kerbyville became a trading center for local miners, as well as loggers and farmers. By 1858, the town had two hotels, several stores, saloons, billiard parlors, and a gristmill.

The county seat was moved to Grants Pass in 1885, and Kerbyville, its name shortened to Kerby, became merely a dot on the road map for most travelers along U.S. Highway 199. But those who stop to look will find several places of interest.

WALKING AND DRIVING AROUND KERBY

The buildings of antiquity in downtown Kerby today are the 1907 two-story Masonic Temple and the 1876 two-story IOOF Hall, both of which have been restored since my first visit in 2003. The most worthwhile buildings, however, are located together beyond downtown at the Kerbyville Museum. The museum contains all manner of historic memorabilia, including musical instruments, mining and assay equipment, and new-old-stock items from the general store in Waldo.

In an outbuilding at the Kerbyville Museum stands an item familiar to federal revenuers during Prohibition: a whiskey still.

The 1871 Stith-Naucke House, next door to the museum, is replete with period furniture and household items. The patriarch of the Naucke family owned and operated a general store, no longer standing, across the street from the house.

Kerby's lovely Laurel Cemetery, located south of town, includes an unusual marker for Pennsylvania native Lyvia Stephens Briggs (1791–1871), identified as a "Daughter of a Revolutionary Soldier." What is unusual is her birth date: Very few Western cemeteries contain the remains of someone born in the eighteenth century.

WHEN YOU GO

Kerby is 27 miles southwest of Grants Pass on U.S. Highway 199. If, however, you are coming from Jacksonville, follow Oregon Highway 238 southwest from town and go through Ruch and Applegate (featuring an 1876 brick schoolhouse on a knoll above town). At 26.7 miles from Jacksonville, Highway 238 enters Murphy and heads north. Instead of following that route, turn left on Murphy Creek Road and make an immediate right onto Southside Road. In 4.1 miles, turn left onto Fish Hatchery Road, which will take you to Wilderville in 4.6 miles. Kerby is 18 miles southwest of Wilderville on U.S. 199.

Coming from Buncom, take Little Applegate Road west for 3 miles, turn north on Applegate Road, and proceed 2.8 miles to Ruch. Follow the above directions from there.

To visit Laurel Cemetery, drive 1.3 miles south from Kerby on U.S. Highway 199 to Laurel Road and turn left. The main entrance to the cemetery is 0.8 of a mile from that turn.

GOLDEN

The town of Golden was organized in 1892, although prospectors and miners had been working nearby Coyote Creek for placer gold sporadically since the 1850s. One of the first buildings erected was a church under the direction of Reverend William Ruble, who was the leader of a Christian sect known as the Campbellites.

Golden's 1904 general store features both a clapboard main building and a board-and-batten addition (left).

Mining prospects improved considerably around the turn of the twentieth century when Ruble's son, S. C. Ruble, invented the Ruble Rock Elevator, a device that removed excess gravel from streambeds. Unlike most mining camps, Golden was

A graceful steeple topped by a spire decorates the Golden Community Church. Reverend William Ruble led the church's first congregation.

not a rowdy place: It featured two churches and no saloons. The town of Placer, four miles southeast, had the nearest watering holes for thirsty miners.

Golden, named for the glittery stuff in Coyote Creek, once had a population of more than a hundred, serving both as a mining town and as a supply center for nearby mines. It received its post office in 1896.

WALKING AROUND GOLDEN

Golden today consists of four buildings. The most photogenic is Reverend Ruble's church, which one source says was rebuilt in 1950. A cemetery next to the church reportedly was created for an episode of the television series *Gunsmoke*, a claim supported by the fact that the topographic map shows no such graveyard. Whatever its origin, the spot now has two real markers, including one for Marion Ellis (1912–1992), one of the area's last miners.

The other buildings in town are Reverend Ruble's badly deteriorating 1894 board-and-batten residence, west and a little north of the church; a former granary and feed store, located east of the church; and, beyond that, the 1904 general store once run by a man named Columbus Bennett.

GOLDEN

WHEN YOU GO

Golden is 50.5 miles northeast of Kerby. From Kerby, take U.S. Highway 199 northeast for 26 miles to Grants Pass. Drive 3 miles through Grants Pass to Interstate 5. Take I-5 17.9 miles north to Exit 76, for Wolf Creek. Turn right. In 0.4 of a mile, follow Coyote Creek Road. Golden is 3.2 miles east along that road.

ACKNOWLEDGMENTS

For historical assistance: Nancy Bell Anderson, Knappton Cove, Washington; Chuck and Stephanie Carpenter, Holden Village, Washington; Dave Chase, Ronald, Washington; Will Craven, Roslyn, Washington; Jay and Barb Phillips, Sumpter Bed and Breakfast Inn, Sumpter, Oregon; Ollie Mae Wilson, Northport, Washington.

For field work assistance: Ethel Bell, George Bell, Rose Hoffman, and Carol Ferguson at Three Valley Gap Chateau, Revelstoke, British Columbia; David Cumming, Fort Steele, British Columbia; Brent Diamond, Holden Village, Washington; Jacci MacDonald, Holden Village, Washington; Jay and Barb Phillips, Sumpter, Oregon; Greg and Mary Ellen Psaltis, Olympia, Washington.

For photographic and technical assistance: Mike Moore, Elgin, Arizona; and John Scott, Tucson, Arizona.

And, perhaps most importantly, for navigation and company on the back roads, grateful thanks to trip companions Reid Psaltis, Nan Allison, and Greg Psaltis.

The Hotel Bellevue's bar has a rather eerie look through the window of its locked entrance at Three Valley Gap, British Columbia.

GLOSSARY

Because so few of the sites in this book involve mining, and because so little evidence of that mining remains, I have used far fewer mining terms in this book than in my previous books. For a more complete glossary, consult *Ghost Towns of the Mountain West* or *Ghost Towns of California*, both published by Voyageur Press.

assay: To determine the value of a sample of ore, in ounces per ton, by testing using a chemical evaluation.

claim: A tract of land with defined boundaries that includes mineral rights extending downward from the surface.

dredge: An apparatus, usually on a flat-bottomed boat, that scoops material out of a river to extract gold-bearing sand or gravel; used in "dredging" or "dredge mining."

hardrock mining: The process in which a primary deposit (see below) is mined by removing ore-bearing rock by tunneling into the earth. Also known as quartz mining, since gold is frequently found in quartz deposits.

headframe: The vertical apparatus over a mineshaft that has cables to be lowered down the shaft for raising either ore or a cage; sometimes called a gallows frame.

hydraulic mining: A method of mining using powerful jets of water to wash away a bank of gold-bearing earth.

mill: A building in which rock is crushed to extract minerals by one of several methods. If this is done by stamps (heavy hammers or pestles), it is a stamp mill. If by iron balls, it is a ball mill. The mill is usually constructed on the side of a hill to utilize its slope—hence, a gravity-fed mill.

mining district: An area of land described (usually for legal purposes) and designated as containing valuable minerals in paying amounts.

ore: A mineral of sufficient concentration, quantity, and value to be mined at a profit.

placer: A waterborne deposit of sand or gravel containing heavier materials like gold, which have been eroded from their original bedrock and concentrated as small particles that can be washed, or "panned," out (see also "secondary deposit," below).

primary deposit: A deposit of gold or other mineral found in its original location.

prospect: Mineral workings of unproven value.

secondary deposit: A deposit of gold or other mineral that has moved from its original location by water. Ore is extracted by placer mining or dredging.

slag: The waste product of a smelter; hence, slag dumps.

smelter: A building or complex in which material is melted in order to separate impurities from pure metal.

strike: The discovery of a primary or secondary deposit of gold or other mineral in sufficient concentration and/or quantity to be mined profitably.

tailings: Waste or refuse left after milling is complete; sometimes used more generally, although incorrectly, to indicate waste dumps.

waste dump: Waste rock, not of sufficient value to warrant milling, that comes out of a mine; usually found immediately outside a mine's entrance.

The headstone of Marion Greene, who died less than two months after her sixth birthday, features a "Lamb of God," a marker frequently used for children's graves. The marker stands in the Granite, Oregon, cemetery.

BIBLIOGRAPHY

Akrigg, G. P. V., and Helen B. Akrigg. *British Columbia Place Names*. 3rd edition. Vancouver: UBC Press, 1997.

Alexander, Ken. *Sumpter, Oregon: A History of the Rise and Decline of a Golden Empire*. Self-published, n.d.

Alotta, Robert I. *Signposts and Settlers: The History of Place Names West of the Rockies*. Chicago: Bonus Books, 1994.

Anderson, Nancy Bell. *The Columbia River's "Ellis Island": The Story of Knappton Cove*. Gearhart, OR: Northwest Heritage Adventures, 2002.

Appelo, Carlton E. *Cottardi Station, Wahkiakum County, Washington*. Deep River, WA: Self-published, 1980.

Barlee, N. L. *Cold Creeks and Ghost Towns of Northeastern Washington*. Blaine, WA, and Surrey, B.C.: Hancock House Publishers and Hancock House Publishers Ltd., 1999.

Basque, Garnet. *Ghost Towns and Mining Camps of the Boundary Country*. Surrey, B.C.: Heritage House Publishing Company Ltd., 1999.

Begg, Alexander. *History of British Columbia*. Toronto: William Briggs, 1894.

Bryan, Liz. *British Columbia: This Favoured Land*. Vancouver: Douglas & McIntyre, 1982.

Burton, Jeffery F., Mary M. Farrell, Florence B. Lord, and Richard W. Lord. *Confinement and Ethnicity: An Overview of World War II Japanese American Relocation Sites*. Tucson, AZ: Western Archeological and Conservation Center (National Park Service, Department of the Interior), 1999.

Carey, Charles Henry. *History of Oregon*. Chicago: The Pioneer Historical Publishing Company, 1922.

Carter, William. *Ghost Towns of the West*. Menlo Park, CA: Lane Magazine and Book Company, 1971 and 1978.

Clarke, S.A. *Pioneer Days of Oregon History*. Vols. 1 and 2. Cleveland: Arthur H. Clark Company, 1905.

Dodds, Gordon B. *Oregon: A Bicentennial History*. New York: W. W. Morton and Company, 1977.

—————*The American Northwest: A History of Oregon and Washington*. Arlington Heights, IL: The Forum Press, 1986.

Eide, Ingvard Henry. *Oregon Trail*. Chicago: Rand McNally and Company, 1972.

Engeman, Richard H. *The Jacksonville Story*. Medford, OR: Southern Oregon Historical Society, 1980 and 1990.

Erickson, Kenneth. *Lumber Ghosts: A Travel Guide to the Historic Lumber Towns of the Pacific Northwest*. Boulder, CO: Pruett Publishing Company, 1994.

Espy, Willard R. *Oysterville: Roads to Grandpa's Village*. Seattle: University of Washington Press, 1977 and 1992.

Fischer, Robin. *Vancouver's Voyage: Charting the Northwest Coast, 1791–1795*. Seattle: University of Washington Press, 1992.

Florin, Lambert. *Alaska and British Columbia Ghost Towns*. Seattle: Superior Publishing Company, 1971.

Fort Clatsop: Rebuilding an Icon. (Written by journalists at the *Daily Astorian*.) Portland, OR: Ooligan Press, 2007.

Forward, Charles N., ed. *British Columbia: Its Resources and People*. Victoria, B.C.: University of Victoria, 1987.

Grants Pass Daily Courier, January 17, 2000.

Gray, William Henry. *The Far Western Frontier: A History of Oregon, 1792–1849*. New York: Arno Press, 1973.

Hill, Larry, ed. *Coal Town Heritage*. Lake Forest Park, WA: Hillcraft Publishing Company, 2002.

Hitchman, Robert. *Place Names of Washington*. Tacoma: Washington State Historical Society, 1985.

Howay, F. W., W. N. Sage, and H. F. Angus. *British Columbia and the United States: The North Pacific Slope from Fur Trade to Aviation*. Toronto: The Ryerson Press, 1992.

Johnston, Hugh J. M., general ed. *The Pacific Province: A History of British Columbia*. Vancouver: Douglas & McIntyre, 1982.

Jones, Herbert E. *Early History of the Big Bend Country*. Wilbur, WA: Big Bend Historical Society, 1963.

Kirk, Ruth, and Carmela Alexander. *Exploring Washington's Past: A Road Guide to History*. Revised ed. Seattle: University of Washington Press, 1995.

Layman, William D. *Native River: The Columbia Remembered*. Pullman, WA: Washington State University Press, 2002.

LeWarne, Charles Pierce. *Washington State*. Revised ed. Seattle: University of Washington Press, 1993.

May, Keith F. *Ghosts of Times Past: A Roadtrip of Eastern Oregon Ghost Towns*. 2nd ed. Kearney, NE: Morris Publishing, 1998.

McArthur, Lewis A. *Oregon Geographic Names*. 4th ed. Portland: Oregon Historical Society, 1974.

Meany, Edmond S. *History of the State of Washington*. New York: The MacMillan Company, 1909.

Miller, Donald C. *Ghost Towns of Washington and Oregon*. Boulder, CO: Pruett Publishing Company, 1977.

Oesting, Marie. *Oysterville: Cemetery Sketches*. Self-published, 1988.

Oregonian, August 30, 1953, and July 7, 2002.

Perry, Adele. *On the Edge of Empire: Gender, Race, and the Making of British Columbia, 1849–1871*. Toronto: University of Toronto Press, 2001.

Phillips, James W. *Washington State Place Names*. Seattle: University of Washington Press, 1971.

Potter, Miles F. *Oregon's Golden Years*. Caldwell, ID: The Caxton Press, 1977.

Rees, Helen Guyton. *Shaniko: From Wool Capital to Ghost Town*. Portland, OR: Binford and Mort Publishing, 1982 and 2002.

Reid, Robert A. *Puget Sound and Western Washington*. Seattle: Robert A. Reid, 1912.

Robinson, J. Lewis, ed. *British Columbia*. Toronto: University of Toronto Press, 1972.

Roy, Patricia E. *The Oriental Question: Consolidating a White Man's Province, 1914–1941*. Vancouver: UBC Press, 2003.

Schmidt, Thomas, and Jeremy Schmidt. *The Saga of Lewis and Clark: Into the Uncharted West*. New York: DK Publishing Company, Inc., 1999.

Scott, James W., and Roland L. DeLorme. *Historical Atlas of Washington*. Norman, OK: University of Oklahoma Press, 1988.

Snowden, Clinton A. *A History of Washington: The Rise and Progress of an American State*. Vol. 1. New York: The Century History Company, 1909.

Statesman Examiner, June 24, 1998.

Sterne, Netta. *Fraser Gold 1858!: The Founding of British Columbia*. Pullman, WA: Washington State University Press, 1998.

Tabor, James Waucop. *Granite and Gold*. Baker, OR: Record-Courier Printers, 1988.

Turnbull, Elsie G. *Ghost Towns and Drowned Towns of the West Kootenay*. Surrey, B.C.: Heritage House Publishing Company Ltd., 2001.

Victor, Frances Fuller. *All Over Oregon and Washington*. San Francisco: John H. Carmany and Co., 1872.

Walker, Dale L. *Pacific Destiny: The Three-Century Journey to the Oregon Country*. New York: Tom Doherty Associates, 2000.

Walter, Donald E., ed. *Lincoln County—A Lasting Legacy*. Davenport, WA: Lincoln County Centennial Committee, 1988.

Weis, Norman. *Ghost Towns of the Northwest*. Caldwell, ID: Caxton Press, 1971.

Wenatchee Daily World, April 26, 1939.

Williams, L. R. *Our Pacific County*. Raymond, WA: *The Raymond Herald*, 1930.

INDEX

Admiralty Head Lighthouse, *30*, 32
Ainsworth, George, 92
Ainsworth Hot Springs, 90, 92–93
Alexander, John B., 31
Alexander's Castle, 31
Allen Hall, 186, *187*
Altoona, *108–9*, 110–11, 113
Altoona Packing Company, 111
Anaconda, 76
Ansorge Hotel, *65, 65*
Antelope, 159–61
Antelope Ancient Order of United Workmen (AOUW) Hall, 160
Antelope Cemetery, 161
Antelope Garage, *159*, 160–61
Antelope Methodist Church, 160, *161*
Antelope school, 161
Astoria Column, 116
Atherton building, 87

B. C. Copper Company Smelter, 79
Balch Hotel, 140, *142*
banks, 41, 59, 60, 67, 198
Barrett House, *79*, 81
Basche's Hardware, 182
Beard's General Merchandise, 67
Beck, Henry, 162
Beekman, Cornelius C., 199–200
Beekman Bank, 199
Beekman House, 199
Bell, Ethel, 82
Bell, Gordon, 82–83
Bennett, Columbus, 211
Blue Mountain Cemetery, *184*, 185
Bodega y Quadra, Juan Francisco, 15
Bodie, 62–63
bootlegging, 46, 64
Bourne, 190–91
Bourne, Jonathan, 190
Boyd, 138–39
Boyd, T. P., 138
Brick Tavern, 41
Briggs, Lyvia Stephens, 208
Buena Vista Cemetery, 26
Bullitt, Logan M., 40

Buncom, 205
Buncom post office, 205
Burns building, 87
Buzzard, Adolphus, 192
Buzzard, Flora, 192

Campbellites, 209
Canadian Pacific Railway, 17, 85, 89, 95
canneries, 110–14, 123, 130
Cape Disappointment Lighthouse, 129
Carbonado, 38
Carlson Block, 37
Casey, Thomas Lincoln, 32
Cementville. *See* Knappton Cove
cemeteries, 26, 31, 37, 43–45, 61, 81, 106, 132, 139, 143, 150–51, 154–55, 162, 165, 171, 193, 200, 204, 208, 211
Chelan, 50–52
Chelan County Museum and Pioneer Village, 48
churches, 26, 38, 43, 69, 81, 123, 131, 145, 150, 165, 172, 174, 188, 193, 199, 209
City Bakery, *96*
Clamshell Railway, 123, 125, 131
Clark, Isaac Alonzo, 130, 132
Clark, William, 15, 107, 112
Cle Elum State Bank, 41
Coal Miners' Memorial and Statue, 41
coal mining, 16, 36, 38, 40–41, 46–47
Coast Artillery Museum, *30*, 31
Columbia River, 15, 99, 107, 110
Columbia River Maritime Museum, 116
Columbia River Packers Association (CRPA), 111
Columbia River Quarantine Station, *114*, 114–15
Columbia Southern Hotel, *156*, 157
Columbia Southern Railroad, 145, 152, 156
copper mining, 51, 76, 79
Corps of Discovery. *See* Lewis and Clark Expedition
Cottardi, Amelio, 111, 113
Cottardi, Baptiste, 110
Cottardi Station, 110–11, *112*, 113
covered bridges, 104, 106
Cracker. *See* Bourne
Cranbrook, 95
Craven, Tom, 44
Craven, Will, 44–45

Crosfield General Merchandise, *144*
Cross Hollows, 156, 158
Curlew, 64–65
Curlew School, *64*, 65
Curlew Store, 65
Customs House, 35

Dairyville. *See* Hardman
Daughters of Progress, 186
Dillier, Otto, 76
Doctor Grice's Painless Dentistry, *95*
dredging, 181, 183, 185, 190–91
Dufur, 138–40
Dufur, Andrew J., 138
Dufur, Enoch, 138
Dufur Historical Society Living History Museum, 139

Ellis, Marion, 211
Emry, Sina, 171
Endersby School, 140, *141*
Espy, Julia, 132
Espy, Robert H., 130–32
Eureka and Epicure Packing Company, 114–15

farming, 16
Federal Mining Company, 205
Federal Mining Company bunkhouse, 205
Field, Pete, 118
Fifteenmile Inn, 139
fishing, 17, 34
Flagler, Daniel Webster, 28
Flora, 192–93
Flora Cemetery, 193
Flora Methodist Episcopal Church, 193
Flora School, *192*, 193
Flora School Education Center, 193
Ford, Henry, 65
Fort Canby, 125, 127–28
Fort Casey, 27–28, 31–33
Fort Casey Inn, *31*, 33
Fort Clatsop, 116–19
Fort Clatsop Memorial Site, 118
Fort Columbia, 125–27
Fort Columbia Barracks Interpretive Center, 127

Fort Columbia commanding officer's quarters, *125*, 127
Fort Columbia Hospital Steward's House, 127
Fort Flagler, 27–29, 33
Fort Flagler hospital, *27*, 28–29
Fort Steele, 94–97
Fort Steele Government Building, *94*
Fort Steele schoolhouse, *96*
Fort Stevens, 120–22
Fort Stevens Historical Site, 120–22
Fort Stevens State Park, 120
Fort Vancouver, 107
Fort Worden, 27–29, 31, 33
Fort Worden commanding officer's quarters, *28–29*, 29
Fort Worden military cemetery, 31
Franklin Lodge, 25
Fraternal Order of Eagles, 37–38
fraternal societies, 25, 37–38, 43, 44, 67, 102, 154–55, 160, 162, 182, 198, 207
Friend, 140, 142–43
Friend, George J., 140
Friend Cemetery, 143
Friend School, 143
fur trading, 15

Galbraith, John, 94
Galbraith's Ferry, 94
Gamble, Robert, 24
general stores, 25–26, 41, 61–62, 65, 67, 76, 92, 106, 132, 140, 186, 211
Giegerich, Henry, 92
Gluggage, James, 197
Golden, 209–11
Golden Cemetery, 211
Golden Community Church, 209, *210*
Golden general store, *209*, 211
gold mining, 16, 51, 62, 92, 94–95, 107, 181, 186, 197, 205, 209
Gold Nugget Saloon, 157
Govan, 68, 70–71
graineries, 138, *139*, 152
grain industry, 107, 138, *139*
grain mills, 138, *139*, 169
Grand Coulee Dam, 112
Grand Hotel, 186
Granite, 186–89

Granite Catholic church, 188
Granite Cemetery, 188
Granite drugstore, 188
Grants Pass, 207
Grass Valley, 144–45, 147–51
Grass Valley Cemetery, *148–49*, 150–51
Grass Valley church, 150
Grass Valley school, *147*, 150
Gray, Robert, 15, 104, 107
Gray's River, 104–6
Gray's River Cemetery, 106
Great Depression, 85
Great Northern Railway, 58, 64, 85
Great Southern Railroad, 138, 140
Greenwood, 76–81
Greenwood cemetery, 81
Greenwood City Hall, 81
Gulley Block, *76*, 81
Gunsmoke, 211

Hardman, 169–71
Hardman Cemetery, 171
Hardman Community Center, *170*, 170
Hardman Independent Order of Odd Fellows (IOOF)
    Hall, *170*, 170
Hardman International Order of Odd Fellows Cemetery, 171
Hardman post office, 170, *171*
Harrington, John Temple Mason, 112
Harris, Johnny, 85–86
Hastings Building, *35*, 35
Hayes, Rutherford B., 199
Heceta, Bruno de, 15
Helphrey, Guy, 64
Holden, 49–53
Holden, James Henry "Harry", 49
Holden Recreation Hall, 52, *53*
Holton, D. S., 206
Holy Trinity Orthodox Christian Church, *18*, 38
Honeymoon Heights, 50
hospitals, 28–29, 52, 127, 182
Hotel Bellevue, *83*, 83
hotels, 26, 33, 38, 52, 67, 76, 79, 83, 92, 97, 145, 157, 186, 199
Hot Springs Camp, 92–93
Howe Sound Mining Company, 49–51

Hudson's Bay Company, 107, 111–12
Hume, George, 110
Hume, Joseph, 110, 114
Hume, Robert, 110
Hume, William, 110, 111
C. B. Hume General Merchants, *82*
Hume Station, 111

Idaho Territory, 16
Ilwaco Railroad & Steam Navigation Company, 123, 125, 131
Imbler, David, 139
Immaculate Conception Catholic Church, 43
International Hotel and Restaurant, *96*, 97
International Order of Odd Fellows Halls, 154, 162, 170, 207

J. B. Fletcher General Merchandise, 92, *93*
J. J. O'Dair Store, 186, *187*
Jackson County Courthouse, 199
Jacksonville, 197–203
Jacksonville butcher shop, 199
Jacksonville Cemetery, 200, *201–3*
Jacksonville City Hall, 199
Jacksonville First Presbyterian Church, 199, *200*
Jacksonville Museum, 199
Jacksonville Redmen's Hall, *197*, 198
Jefferson, Thomas, 15, 116
Jefferson County Courthouse, *34*, 34–35
Jeremiah Nunan House, *198*, 203
Johnson, Frank, 192
Johnson Meadow. *See* Flora

Kaslo & Slocan Railway, 89
Kendrick Mercantile Company, *66*, 67
Kent, 144–45, 152–55
Kent Cemetery, 154–55
Kent grain elevators, 152, 154
Kent Odd Fellows Cemetery, 154–55
Kent Independent Order of Odd Fellows (IOOF) Hall, 154
Kent school, 153
Kent service station, 152–53
Kerby, 206–8
Kerby, James, 206
Kerby International Order of Odd Fellows Hall, 207
Kerby Masonic Temple, 207

Kerbyville. *See* Kerby
Kerbyville Museum, 207
Klondike Gold Rush, 17
Knapp, Jabez Burrell, 114
Knappton Cove, 114–15
Knappton Cove Heritage Center, *114*, 114–15
Kootenay Post. *See* Fort Steele
K. Kubli Building, 198

Lake Chelan, 52
Laurel Cemetery, 208
lead mining, 95
Lewis, Meriwether, 15, 107
Lewis and Clark Expedition, 15, 107, 116–18
Lewis and Clark Interpretive Center, 119, 128–29
Liberty Hotel, 67
lighthouses, 30–31, 128–29
Locust Grove, 145
Locust Grove United Brethren Church, 145, *146*
logging, 16–17
Lonerock, 165–68
Lonerock Cemetery, 165
Lonerock Community Hall, 165, *168*
Lonerock jail, *165*, 165
Lonerock Methodist church, 165, *166–67*
Lonerock school, 165
Louisiana Purchase, 15
Lucerne, 50, 52
lumber, 22, 34, 67, 179
Lutheran Bible Institute, 51

Mack, Julius, 132–33
Maiwaldt, Clara, 185
Maiwaldt, Ernst, 185
Marrowstone Island, 28
Masonic lodges, 67, 182
Mayville, 162–64
Mayville Cemetery, 162, *164*
Mayville garage, 162, *163*
Mayville Independent Order of Odd Fellows (IOOF) Hall, 162, *163*
McArthur, W. E., 78–79
McGowan, 123
McGowan, Patrick J., 123
Meacham, George, 58

Medford, 198
Megler, 123
Megler, Joseph D., 123
Molson, 58–61
Molson, George, 58
Molson Cemetery, 61
Molson schoolhouse, *60*, 60
Molson State Bank, *59*, 60
Molson Trading Company, *61*, 61
Moro, 144, 145, 147
Moro school, 147
Mount Pisgah Presbyterian Church, 43
museums, 26, 28, 31, 60, 65, 84, 89, 92, 97, 102, 116, 121, 127, 139, 147, 182, 199, 207

Chief Nahcati, 132
National Historic Districts, 41, 102
National Historic Landmarks, 198
National Register of Historic Places, 38, 115, 121, 130, 131, 140, 145
New Caledonia. *See* British Columbia
Nibley Lumber Company sawmill, 179
Nikkei Internment Memorial Centre, 77
Northern Exposure, 40–41
Northern Pacific Railway, 17, 36, 40, 70
North Head Lighthouse, 128–29
Northport, 66–67
Northport News, 66
Northport Smelting and Refining Company, 66–67, 67
Nunan, Jeremiah, 203

An Officer and a Gentleman, 29
Of Sea and Shore Museum, 26
Order of the Redmen, 102
Oregon & California Railroad, 198
Oregon Historical Society, 118
Oregon Steam Navigation Company, 107
Oregon Territory, 15
Oregon Trail, 15
Oregon Trunk railroad, 157
Orth, John, 199
J. Orth Building, 199
Orth House, 199
Oskaloosa Hotel, 145

INDEX

oyster fishing, 130–31
Oysterville, 130–33
Oysterville Cemetery, 132
Oysterville Church, *130–31*, 131
Oysterville General Store, 132

Pacific Hotel, 79, 81
Peter Rabbit grocery store, 50
Petersen, Hans, 111
Petersen, Nellie, 111
Pillar Rock, 110, 112–13
Pillar Rock Packing Company, 112
Pioneer Drug Store, *97*
Point Wilson Lighthouse, 31
Pool, James, 197
Pope, A. J., 22, 24, 26
Port Gamble, 22–26
Port Gamble community hall, 25
Port Gamble General Store and Office, *23*, 25
Port Gamble Historic Museum, 26
Port Townsend, 34–35
Potlatch Grange Hall, *69–70*, 69
Prohibition, 46, 64
Puget Hotel, 26
Puget Sound, 15, 22, 24
Pulliam, Dora, 113
Pulliam, Jim, 113
Pulliam, Leif, 111, 113

Quimper Peninsula, 29

R. H. Espy residence, 131
railroads, 17, 34, 145, 169, 177, 179. *See also individual railroads*
Railway Standard Watchmaker & Jewellery Store, 82
Rajneesh. *See* Antelope
Rajneesh, Bhagwan Shree, 159–60
ranching, 16
Raw Dog. *See* Hardman
Rebekah Lodge Community Cemetery, 139
Retallack, 90, *91*
Retallack, John L., 90
Richmond, 172–75
Richmond Methodist church, 172, *173*, 174
Richmond school, 172, 174

Ritchie, Willis A., 35
River Life Interpretive Center, 102, *103*
Rogue River Valley Railway, 198
Rollins, Josephine, 206
Ronald, 46–47
Rosberg, Christian, 104
Rosburg, 104, 106
Rosburg cemetery, *105*, 106
Rosburg School, 106
Rosburg Store, 106
Roslyn, 40–45
Roslyn African American Masonic Cemetery, 44
Roslyn City Cemetery, 43–45, *44*, *45*
Roslyn old company store, 41
Ruble, S. C., 210
Ruble, William, 209

Sacagawea, 117
Sacred Heart Catholic Church, *80*, 81
salmon fishing, 110–12, 123
salteries, 111–12
Saltmarsh, Mary E., 204
Sandon, 85–89
Sandon, John, 85
Sandon City Hall, *88*, 89
Sandon Museum, *85–86*, 89
sandstone, 36–37
sawmills, 24, *49*, 52, 62, 66, 76, 179
Scarborough House, 127
Schernechau, August, 156
schools and schoolhouses, 37–38, 47, 52, 60, 62, 65, 70, 96, 102, 106, 140, 143, 145, 147, 150, 153, 158, 165, 172, 174, 186, 193
Schreiber House, 139, *140*
Searchlight Powerhouse, *126*, 127
Seattle Pacific University, 33
Shaniko, 144–45, 156–58
Shaniko City Hall, 157
Shaniko Hotel, *156*, 157
Shaniko school, 158
Shaniko water tower, 158
Shaniko wool shed, 157
Sheela, Ma Anand, 160
Sherling, Ethel, 61

Sherling, Harry A., 61
Sherman, 68–70
Sherman, George, 69
Sherman, William Tecumseh, 199
Sherman County Courthouse, 147
Sherman County Historical Museum, 147
Sherman Presbyterian Church, *68*, 69
Silver Ledge Hotel, 92
silver mining, 51, 85, 90, 95, 107
Silversmith Hydroelectric Generating Station, 89
Silvery Slocan, 85
Simpkins, Myra E., 203
Skamokawa, 102–3
Skamokawa Redmen Hall, 102, *103*
Skamokawa schoolhouse, 102, *103*
Slocan Mercantile, 85–86, 89
smelters, 66–67, 79
Snake River, 107
Spencer, Mary A., 69
Spokane Falls & Northern Railroad, 66
St. Anthony's Catholic Church, *97*
St. Jude's Anglican Church, 81
St. Mary's Catholic Church, 123, *124*
St. Patrick Mission, 65
St. Paul's Episcopal Church, *24*, 26
Stahlberger, August, 122
Stearn, A. T., 132
A. T. Stearn residence, 131–33
Steele, Samuel Benfield, 94
Sterlingville Cemetery, 204
Stevens, Isaac Ingalls, 120
Stith-Naucke House, *206–7*, 208
Stump Dodger railroad, 177, 181
Sumpter, 181–85
Sumpter Dredge No. 3, 183, 185
Sumpter General Hospital, 182
Sumpter Municipal Museum, 182, *183*
Sumpter Supply, 182, 183
Sumpter Trading Post, 182
Sumpter Valley Railway, 177, 181–82

Table Rock City. *See* Jacksonville
Tabor, Albert Gallatin, 186, 188
Tabor, James Waucop "Walkie", 190
Tabor, Margaret, 190

Talbot, William C., 22, 24, 26
Tanger, Carl A., 132–33
Teekalet. *See* Port Gamble
Thomas Wansboro Battery, 29
Three Valley Gap, 82–84
Three Valley Lake Chateau, 82
"Triangle of Fire", 27

United States Hotel, 199

Vancouver, George, 15
Vancouver Island, 16

Waldron School, 174
Walker, Cyrus, 22
Walters, J., 64
War Games Building, 121
Wasa Hotel, 97
Wasco, 144–45
Wasco Elementary School, 145
Wasco railroad depot, 145
Washington Central Railroad, 70
Washington Family Ranch, 161
Washington Hotel, *38*, 38
Waucop, Robert W., 186
Wenatchee Daily World, 50
Whidbey Island, 31
Whitney, 179–80
Whitney Cemetery, 180
Wilkeson, 36–39
Wilkeson, Samuel, 36
Wilkeson Cemetery, 37, *39*
Wilkeson Grocery, 37
Wilkeson School, *37*, 38
Wilson, Jerry M., 154–55
Windsor Hotel, *77*, 79
winemaking, 46
Winston Camp, 50
Wood, Robert, 76
wool, 156–57
Worden, John L., 29
World War I, 85
World War II, 51, 77–78, 81, 86, 120

zinc mining, 51

ABOUT THE AUTHOR AND PHOTOGRAPHER

PHILIP VARNEY is the author of eight ghost town guidebooks, including *Ghost Towns of the Mountain West, Ghost Towns of California, Arizona's Ghost Towns and Mining Camps,* and *New Mexico's Best Ghost Towns.*

Varney visited his first ghost town—Central City, Colorado—at the age of eleven and has been an enthusiast ever since. A former high school English teacher and department chairman, he has toured and photographed more than six hundred ghost towns throughout the American West.

In addition to his ghost town books, Varney has authored a book on bicycle tours of southern Arizona, was a contributing writer for Insight Guide's *Wild West,* and has been a contributor to *Arizona Highways* magazine. *True West* magazine has honored Philip Varney as one of the two "Best Living Photographers of the West."

Philip Varney lives in Tucson, Arizona.